The First-Time Horse and Pony Owner

KT-405-572

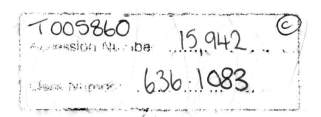

T005860
Accession Number .....15,942..... ©
Class Number .636.:1083.

The First-Time Horse and Pony Owner

Tricia Johnson, BHSAI

Foreword by Lionel Dunning

SWAN·HILL
PRESS

Copyright © 1992 by Tricia Johnson

First published in the UK in 1989 by Pelham Books. This edition first published in 1992 by Swan Hill Press, an imprint of Airlife Publishing Ltd.

British Library Cataloguing in Publication Data
A catalogue record for this book is available
from the British Library.

ISBN 1 85310 336 5

All rights reserved. No part of this book may be reproduced or transmitted in any form or by any means, electronic or mechanical including photocopying, recording or by any information storage and retrieval system, without permission from the Publisher in writing.

Printed in England by Livesey Ltd., Shrewsbury.

Swan Hill Press
an imprint of Airlife Publishing Ltd.,
101 Longden Road, Shrewsbury SY3 9EB.

CONTENTS

ACKNOWLEDGEMENTS

My grateful thanks go to: my long-suffering husband Michael, without whose sacrifices I would not be able to keep my own, dearly loved horses;

My equally long-suffering parents who encouraged my involvement with horses every step of the way, despite being totally unable to understand it;

Mrs Janet Sturrock (FBHS) who gave me as thorough a training as anyone could wish for at The Wharf.

The photographs are reproduced by kind permission of *Horse and Pony* Magazine, EMAP Pursuit Publications Ltd. The line drawings are by Dianne Breeze based on roughs supplied by Sean Denning.

FOREWORD

Riding and owning horses is one of the fastest growing leisure activities in the world today. As a trainer of competition riders I frequently encounter people new to the game who, although well-meaning, just do not realise the commitment they have undertaken.

They take advice – often conflicting – wherever they can, and end up being thoroughly confused; either that or they just trust to luck to see them through.

Everyone has to start somewhere; many of today's top riders come from non-horsey backgrounds so were, at one point, 'first-time' owners.

This book is a comprehensive basic guide to owning a horse for the first time, and contains many useful tips which normally only come the hard way – with experience. It is written in a down-to-earth style which not only instructs but explains.

The only advice I would add from the riding side is to find a good professional instructor, and stay with him or her.

All the successful overseas competitors have their own trainers who mould each individual rider's career from start to finish, and since their reputation stands or falls by the rider's performance, the trainers have a vested interest in 'getting it right'.

The same applies to schooling problem horses – go to someone who really knows, and don't rely on a succession of well-meaning friends offering different ideas.

With this book, you will be set on the right track to begin with; it is then up to you to decide whether you want to expand and deepen your knowledge, and perhaps even take up serious competing.

LIONEL DUNNING

INTRODUCTION

The pleasure to be derived from owning a horse or pony is incalculable, but 'first-time' owners quickly discover that there is much more to it than simply riding.

It is a sad fact that the majority of cruelty cases arise, not through wilful neglect, but as a result of ignorance – and this book is intended to provide you, the 'first-time' owner, with a basic guide to the requirements and responsibilities involved.

For this reason, the story begins long before a horse ever arrives at your establishment. Understanding the commitment, preparing the facilities which will be needed and knowing what to look for in a prospective purchase will all help to set you on the right path to successful ownership.

Subsequent chapters deal with the day-to-day management of the horse, outlining its needs and capabilities. Each horse is an individual, so there can be few hard-and-fast rules which apply rigidly to each and every one. For every 'rule' put forward, you can be sure that someone, somewhere, has successfully done the exact opposite – and got away with it. However, by following the basic principles outlined in this book you can avoid many of the pitfalls which would otherwise arise.

Common sense is the key above all, coupled with a basic knowledge which will deepen and expand with experience. Things which come naturally to someone born and brought up with horses may seem totally foreign to a new owner, and it is for this reason that I have attempted to explain not only what should be done but why.

Not all owners have unlimited resources in terms of time, money and facilities, and I feel it is important to understand where short cuts can be made safely.

Wherever possible, I have suggested solutions to problems which habitually crop up, and I have tried to guide the reader through the maze of available information in a straightforward, logical manner. It is all too easy to be 'blinded by science', and particularly so with the study of horses, but this book will, I hope, explain all you need to know to establish a rewarding relationship with your first horse.

TRICIA JOHNSON

CHAPTER 1

Counting the Cost

The cost of keeping a horse or pony can vary enormously, depending on such factors as: the type of animal; the purpose for which it is kept; the area in which you live; whether you can keep it yourself or at livery; whether it is kept at grass, stabled or both – and many more.

A thoroughbred competition horse, for example, will probably cost twice as much to keep as a family-type cob living out; livery charges vary from one area to another too, as do veterinary charges, blacksmiths' fees and so on. The cost of feed will depend on how, when and where it is bought as well as the individual horse's requirements – so it really is impossible to say exactly how much a horse will cost to keep.

The best thing to do is make a rough estimate from all the factors listed below, applying your individual circumstances.

Keep

The cost of renting grazing, as I have said, will vary from one part of the country to another – and not always logically.

Certain areas in the south of England have a very high horse population, and grazing is at a premium, but balanced against this is the fact that there is much more land laid to grass than in intensively agricultural counties. In general, though, grazing is cheaper in the Midlands and North.

With horse-owning gaining popularity year by year, and comparatively small parcels of land for sale being at a premium both in terms of price and availability, it is worth bearing in mind that most farmers are only too well aware that they have the upper hand, and it is only very few horse owners who are in a position to haggle over rent, facilities, etc.

If you are looking for livery, it certainly pays to shop around. Do-it-yourself livery is becoming increasingly popular, and it is the cheapest form. This is an arrangement whereby the owner undertakes to look after the horse on a day-to-day basis, paying the yard for the use of a stable and/or grazing.

The yard may also provide straw or other bedding, and occasionally hay, for which you pay extra. As a new owner – and especially if you are also new to the area – this arrangement could suit you well, at least until you find your feet and get to know the local suppliers. However, you must make sure that any hay fed to your horse is of good quality.

Another potential cost-cutter is 'working' livery. Under this scheme, you pay a reduced amount if the yard has permission to use your horse for their own purposes – as in a riding school for example.

This can work very well; it would mean that your horse is exercised regularly – a godsend if you are in a full-time job, or cannot ride during the week in winter.

Equally, however, it has its disadvantages – you must be sure in your own mind that your horse is not overworked, or worked irregularly, or that you won't arrive to ride at weekends and find that the horse is already booked, or even too tired.

Yards offering livery advertise in horsey magazines, or can be found by word of mouth. The vet, blacksmith, riding club, Pony Club are worthwhile contacts.

Good quality hay is a must, and the cost will vary from one area to another and depend on the quantity bought, and the time of year, and, of course, the weather. The best time to buy is during the haymaking season – May to June – direct from the farmer, off the field. If you wait until later in the year and have to buy from a merchant, you will find it much more expensive – and after Christmas it may well be in short supply too! Wet weather during haymaking will result in high prices, whereas in a good year hay will be cheaper.

From October/November until April/May, even the best grass will have very little feed value, so hay must be fed – even if the horse is not in work. This hay will also play a large part in keeping the horse warm as the digestive process generates 'inner warmth', so should ideally be fed *ad lib*. A family cob, living out, will eat around half a bale of hay a day depending on the horse's age, condition and the amount of work it is expected to do. In your calculations, allow three and a half bales a week for six months and then one bale a week for a further two months to be on the safe side – it is better to over- rather than underestimate.

Straw is also best bought off the field; in this case after harvest which will be August-September. A horse stabled at night through the winter will use around three bales a week.

Shavings and other commercially produced bedding materials such as shredded paper, sawdust or peat are normally available throughout the year and can be obtained from agricultural merchants or specialist suppliers.

'Hard' food such as oats, cubes, other cereals and bran or chaff will be necessary if the horse is to be ridden – and should be fed through the winter in any case to maintain condition. There are now several 'coarse mixes' on the market which, together with hay, provide a balanced diet. They do tend to work out more expensive than buying, say, rolled oats, cubes and bran separately, but they save a lot of trouble and eliminate guesswork from the diet.

An added advantage is that they contain amounts of several different cereals and minerals which might otherwise be difficult to incorporate. They also come in pre-determined types for different circumstances, such as young stock, horses in light work, competition horses, brood mares and so on.

Mineral supplements and salt licks are also necessary, especially for very young and/or very old horses.

Farrier

His services will be required every six to eight weeks, whether the horse is shod or not, and his charges will vary depending on whether the feet are just trimmed or need a new set of shoes. There will be an extra charge for travelling if he comes out to your premises.

Wormers

The horse will require worming every six to ten weeks, and the vet will advise on cost. (You should not use the same brand every time as resistance to one particular type can be built up over a period of time.)

Vet

At the very least your horse will need one visit a year from the vet to administer the annual tetanus vaccination, and have its teeth checked. The cost of this will vary depending on where you live and how far the vet has to travel. This cannot be claimed on any horse insurance policy, as it is not classed as accident or injury.

Tack and equipment

Not only must you consider the initial cost of buying the necessary saddlery etc. (and there is a lot more to it than just saddle and bridle), you must also maintain it in good repair – even the best cared-for tack can break, and accidents to such items as New Zealand rugs can prove costly to put right.

Insurance

It is always as well to have the horse insured, even if you only have the basic policy which covers you for theft or loss through straying and death of the horse, as this will also include public liability cover.

For an extra premium, you can also have cover for vets' fees, theft of or damage to saddlery and tack, personal accident cover and loss or damage to a trailer.

Any reputable insurance broker will be able to advise you on the best company and policy for your circumstances. Remember, the cheapest is not usually the best, and some insurance companies are notoriously difficult when it comes to a claim.

Freeze-marking

This is an extra expense, but is worth every penny. Despite the escalating number of horse thefts, *not one* freeze-marked horse or pony has been permanently lost. The coded number marked on the horse's back is held in a central registry, and an automatic reward is posted at all the ports and slaughter houses in the country. It is virtually impossible for a thief to dispose of a stolen branded horse – alive or dead.

It is a sad fact that the vast majority of unmarked stolen horses and ponies are rarely still alive twenty-four hours after they have been taken. It is foolhardy to imagine that it can't happen to you – because the statistics show otherwise; and after the event it will be too late.

The cost varies depending on the number of horses or ponies to be marked in one session, so it is worth organising a group to reduce an individual owner's outlay. A contact address can be found at the end of this book.

Membership of clubs and societies

Membership of the British Horse Society, Pony Club or local riding club should be considered. Apart from the obvious benefits like instructional sessions, rallies, shows, etc., it also means that you have someone to turn to if you have any problems; membership fees vary according to the organisation, but BHS membership also includes automatic third-party liability insurance.

Transport

If you intend to do any amount of competing, you will need horse transport of some kind. Hiring a box for a day is prohibitively expensive if it has to be done more than three or four times a year, and a secondhand trailer of your own may well solve your transport problem. A trailer also has many other uses – not necessarily connected with transporting horses. Good secondhand trailers are widely available and the cost will depend on the age, make and condition.

Your car also has to be considered – it may not be 'man' enough to tow a trailer, and it must be remembered that engine size isn't everything. Since most garages are usually concerned with selling a particular car, it is worth contacting one of the national motoring associations, or the BHS, for advice on a suitable towing vehicle.

As far as cost is concerned, you will find that, in general, a car which is capable of towing a horse trailer will be costlier to buy and maintain (as well as being less economical on fuel) than an average small family saloon. Personal experience has shown that diesel cars are well worth considering.

When you have worked out what you think the horse or pony will cost to keep, you should then add on an extra ten per cent and look on the black side. There will always be unforeseen expenses no matter how carefully you try to budget.

If your funds will only run to the exact amount of your estimate, you would be wise to shelve the idea of ownership for the time being. Instead try to share a friend's horse, and wait for your circumstances to improve. This, believe it or not, will save a considerable amount of worry in the long run.

You will probably have noticed that I have made no mention of the initial cost of buying the horse – this really is the least of your worries, and in fact it is very often possible to obtain one on long-term loan, especially in the case of children's ponies, which are all too quickly outgrown.

CHAPTER 2

Gaining Practical Experience

Assuming your budget has worked out favourably and you have decided that you want your own horse, you should stop and consider your own capabilities before finally committing yourself.

You will, presumably, have been taught to ride, and have some experience of grooming and tacking up. However, if this is the sum total of your practical knowledge you will save yourself a lot of worry, and avoid making drastic mistakes, if you take the time to learn more about stable routine and procedures, basic handling techniques and so on before you take the plunge and buy your horse.

Obviously you can learn much from textbooks, but really there is no substitute for practical experience, and this can be gained in a number of ways.

You could ask a horse-owning friend if you could tag along for a couple of weeks to watch how things are done, or you could offer to help out at a local riding school with the mundane jobs – mucking out and cleaning tack for example. Working at a commercial establishment would provide the opportunity of observing several different horses and ponies, each with its own individual temperament which may require slightly differing treatment; you would also be taught the correct and most practical way of coping with various situations, and the proprietor would probably be only too pleased to have the extra help – unpaid of course – especially if you explain your reasons.

Your riding should be of a sufficiently high standard to cope with any situation you are likely to meet, or any mild forms of misbehaviour on the part of your horse, but there is no necessity to be a top-class cross-country rider or an expert in dressage in order to enjoy safe hacking around the countryside. If you subsequently decide to compete, you can take lessons on your own horse to improve your standard of riding, and the horse will be educated at the same time.

Although horses are first and foremost individuals, you will find certain similarities in behaviour which are fairly common to all, and if you learn to recognise these and deal with them, it will be valuable experience when it comes to dealing with your own horse. Having said that, you will always find an exception to every rule, but for example not many horses would be too impressed if a large paper or plastic bag were to blow across the road in front of them, or if another horse were to suddenly rush up behind them. Some horses will shy at anything and everything, while others will completely ignore some of the most 'horrifying' objects and situations – only to shoot across the road if a leaf rustles. These individual quirks can only be anticipated by experience – getting to know the individual horse – but in the first instance it is better to play safe and avoid the obvious hazards if possible.

Remember that, if you are frightened, this will communicate itself to the horse which will then react in any one of a number of ways. Some horses will react to fear on the part of a rider or handler by immediately panicking – whether they can see a cause or not; an old children's pony may well be used to nervous riders and choose to ignore them completely.

The main thing is to be firm, but kind. Approach a strange horse with caution, but don't treat it like an unexploded bomb which is about to go off. If you are leading a horse past something of which it is afraid, stay level with its shoulder and don't try to pull it along. Talking to a frightened horse in a calm, confident but soothing voice will work wonders – shouting and bluster on the other hand, will only make matters worse.

If a horse misbehaves, you have to punish it. Don't overdo the reprimand but equally, nothing will be gained by giving it a little tap with a whip and saying, 'Oh, you are a naughty boy!' in a childish voice. One sharp rap with a riding crop accompanied by a growl and the horse will realise that it has done wrong. You may rap the offending part of the horse's anatomy – for example, if it kicks at you, you should rap it on the thigh, but *never* hit a horse on or near the head, or on the bony parts of the legs. The object is exactly the same as with naughty children – you are aiming to make your displeasure felt, but you do not want to inflict any damage. It is an unfortunate fact that horses owned and handled predominantly by women tend to be generally naughtier than those handled by men – not because the men hit them harder, but usually because the horse has learned the limitations of a woman's power over it, and it has been allowed to get away with too many minor transgressions. Some habits start off by being amusing, but if not checked in the early stages will develop into major nuisances – and in some cases become downright dangerous.

Remember also that horses are physically much stronger than humans – our only advantage lies in our superior brain power, which is why the horse *must* learn 'who's boss'.

There are very few horses which are really evil, but there are many which are naughty, usually through having been spoiled as a youngster. The major problem is to decide whether the horse is being naughty because it is frightened, confused or just plain disobedient. This is not always as easy as you might think; a horse can start off by being genuinely frightened of an object or situation, for example a tractor or large vehicle, but if it is allowed to have its own way, the initial fear will be replaced by the knowledge that certain circumstances can be used as a good excuse to play up.

Obviously, beating a frightened horse will achieve nothing – except to increase its fear – so patience and perseverance have to be the order of the day. You must insist, gently but firmly, that your instructions are obeyed.

Working with and observing several different horses in this way will also teach you the basic techniques of everyday management, from catching the horse in the field, to grooming and tacking up etc. ready to ride out.

Some yards impose the rule that you should not give horses titbits; this is because it encourages them to look for food whenever someone approaches. Some horses get quite nasty when none is forthcoming, biting, pushing and generally being bad-tempered. I believe an exception to this rule should be made when you catch a horse in a field, when a titbit can be offered as a reward. If this (and possibly after a horse is loaded into a horsebox or trailer) is the only occasion, it does not matter if the horse comes to expect it. This small incentive can save hours of frustration when a loose horse has no intention of being caught.

While you are gaining experience on the practical side, take every opportunity to watch various horsey procedures – visits to or from the farrier and vet, for example, or loading horses ready for travel; you will then have some idea of what to expect when you are on your own.

Don't be afraid to ask questions, and if you don't fully understand something, ask for the explanation to be repeated. Horses are not pieces of machinery which can be put on one side while you go off and look something up in a book – situations have to be dealt with as and when they arise, so it makes sense to be as well prepared as possible.

CHAPTER 3

Stable-Kept or Grass-Kept?

It is certainly much cheaper to keep a horse or pony at grass all year round rather than having it stabled, but in fact the animal will be much happier, and probably healthier, if it lives out. This is partly due to the fact that the grass-kept horse is in a much more natural environment; to a large extent it can regulate its own exercise and diet, and provided that there is some form of shade and shelter available, there is no reason why most horses – and certainly ponies – cannot stay out even in the winter. Any infections, too, are less liable to spread among stabled horses.

For successful all-year-round keep, one horse will require about 1½–2 acres; one pony 1–1½ acres. Two horses will need around 3 acres, and for two ponies 2 acres should be adequate. For more than two horses an allowance of 1 acre each should be made, and more than two ponies should have ½–¾ acre each. These figures must be regarded as approximate, since much will depend on the type and suitability of the field.

The only weather conditions to worry about are wet and cold together; frost and snow in themselves are not harmful – in fact most horses and ponies enjoy playing in the snow as much as any child. The hairs of the coat trap 'layers' of air between them to conserve body heat, and there will be a shine which no amount of grooming alone can achieve.

When it is wet and cold, though, the coat becomes flattened, and an unprotected horse can easily become thoroughly chilled.

In these circumstances, if the horse is to stay out at night, it must have a New Zealand rug to keep its back and loins dry. This type of rug consists of a tough waterproof outer with a warm blanket lining, and is specifically designed for wear in the field.

From October/November until April/May the horse will require a plentiful supply of hay in the field as the grass will have little or no feed value, and hay should also be made available to horses which are turned out only during the day, as in the winter months an abrupt change in diet from hay eaten while in the stable overnight to frozen grass can cause colic.

Hay, in fact, plays a vital part in keeping a horse warm during very cold weather, due to the fermentation which takes place in the gut, but even the small amount of grass eaten through the winter will aid the digestion of the oats which probably form the basis of its hard feed ration.

Another advantage of keeping the horse out as much as possible is that it will usually present a much more relaxed and co-operative frame of mind than its stabled counterpart, and this is particularly important when the ground is treacherous. Whereas you may well find yourself taking your life in your hands when taking a stabled horse out for the first time after a spell of enforced inactivity, this is not usually the case with one who has been accustomed to the freedom of its field.

Horses are naturally gregarious animals, and, if left to their own devices for hours on end, shut in a stable away from their companions – human as well as equine – will tend to develop bad habits and vices arising through sheer boredom. Some of these are annoying rather than dangerous, but others can not only pose a threat to their health, but also are classed as technical unsoundnesses. (See Chapter 20.)

The diet of a stabled horse has to be carefully monitored to avoid a build-up of protein in the blood during a period of inactivity. Two fairly common examples of this were both known as 'Monday morning disease' in the old days, as they commonly afflicted horses which were brought out for work on a Monday morning after having spent the Sunday idle in their stable but on full oat ration. These are now more frequently called by their proper names – lymphangitis and azoturia (see Chapter 15), but are rarely seen in grass-kept horses.

The horses' feet will benefit from being out at grass, as the constant, albeit gentle, exercise will help to keep them cool, and the natural goodness in the grass the horse eats will ensure a healthy, vigorous growth of horn.

The extra grooming required to make the horse look presentable is more than offset by all these factors. In any case, in the winter it is not necessary to remove all the mud from its body before you ride – just make sure that the areas in direct contact with the tack are clean. In the summer, if you intend to compete, a bath the night before the show, followed by a thorough grooming in the morning, will produce an immaculate animal, and it will probably be a lot better-behaved too.

If you intend to do any amount of work through the winter, you will find that the horse starts to sweat heavily in its thick winter coat, and if this is so, it should be clipped, as condition will be lost very rapidly through sweating. If a partial clip such as a trace clip or 'Pony Club' clip (the coat is removed from the belly and the underside of the neck) is carried out, the horse will still be able to live out, but in a

New Zealand rug, as these clips were specifically designed to horses and ponies to work comfortably while out at grass.

Most horses and ponies will soon let you know if they are cold and want to come in to a stable, either by such obvious ploys as standing by the field gate looking thoroughly sorry for themselves, or standing with their backs hunched, tails clamped down and backs towards the wind.

In the Yorkshire Dales, and indeed many other parts of the country, it is quite common practice to leave even thoroughbreds and youngstock out in the fields all winter without rugs, and they seem to come to no harm; the old horsemen maintain that horses are far less likely to take a chill from living out than when kept stabled, and they may well have a point. Personally I would recommend that youngsters up to the age of two and older thoroughbreds should be stabled at night in severe weather. This is mainly because they need more attention than horses in the prime of life, and particularly in the case of youngstock, the food they eat is required for growth and strength and not just for keeping warm.

Children's ponies should always – with only a very few exceptions – be kept out. Artful at the best of times, they quickly pick up bad habits if kept stabled, and a child is very often not physically strong enough to keep a fractious pony under complete control when it has other ideas.

If a horse or pony is to be kept on its own and you really do think it is lonely, you should consider finding some company for it. Many people keep retired sea-side donkeys for this purpose, but you *must* make sure that the donkey is regularly wormed with a preparation which will kill lungworm, as donkeys are invariably carriers of this parasite which, untreated, is extremely dangerous to horses.

A sample of a donkey's dung should be given to your vet for a worm count at least twice a year to be on the safe side.

Apart from this, donkeys make excellent companions for horses, and are often to be found travelling with racehorses to keep them calm. Another animal worth considering is the goat. A determined billy goat is more than able to hold its own with a horse or pony, and it will also help to keep the paddock tidy by eating grasses which the horse dislikes. Strategically tethered next to patches of untidy grass or weeds, a goat can transform the appearance of a field in a surprisingly short space of time.

Domestic geese are another idea for companionship. They cannot fly so are easily contained, and they make excellent guards. If anyone should come prowling around the field at night, for example, the neighbourhood would be in for a rude awakening.

Companionship seems to be more important for horses than for ponies; the latter seem to adapt very well to living alone, but horses will often mope – or even become hell-bent on escape. The herd instinct remains very strong in some individuals, and if the horse or pony shows signs of needing a companion, measures must be taken immediately since the safety – as well as the health – of the horse may be in danger.

CHAPTER 4

A Suitable Field

Finding a field to rent

When you start looking for a field to rent, especially if you are new to an area, arm yourself with an Ordnance Survey map and drive around first to familiarise yourself with the roads and lanes, so at least you will have some idea of the lie of the land and can see what is available.

If there are very few grass fields in the area, you will know that the chances of being able to pick and choose are slim. If, on the other hand, there seem to be several smallish grass fields with relatively few horses in them, you may stand a better chance – but, unfortunately, farmers will always have the upper hand, and generally they know it.

Write down the locations of any suitable fields you come across and make enquiries at the nearest houses to find out the owner's name. Bear in mind that a field five or six miles away from your home is not necessarily a problem in summer, but could well prove a different story in winter when daylight is limited or the roads are treacherous.

The district commissioner of the local branch of the Pony Club, the secretary of a local riding club, the proprietor of a riding school, farriers and vets are all people in a position to have an idea where grazing might be found – even the agricultural department of local estate agents can sometimes come up trumps. If several villages fall within the scope of your travels, it is often a good idea to call in at the local pubs and make enquiries there.

If the first farmer you approach has no grazing to offer, ask him if he knows of others you can try. If he suggests a field, make an appointment to go and look at it with him. Try to take someone with you when you go, as two pairs of eyes (and ears) are better than one. You then have a witness while terms and conditions are discussed, so any future arguments over who said what can easily be resolved. (Farmers rarely want to put anything in writing.)

At this point establish exactly who is to be responsible for the maintenance of fences, ditches, gates, etc., and make sure that if the field is not quite large enough for your needs, he would be willing to rent you additional grazing for short periods when required. It is

THE LIBRARY
BISHOP BURTON COLLEGE
BEVERLEY HU17 8QG
TEL: 0964 550481 Ex: 227

better to sort this out in advance rather than leaving it until there isn't a blade of grass left in your paddock and risking the possibility of an outright refusal.

Sharing a field

Check whether the farmer would want to graze other stock in with your horse or pony. There can be both advantages and disadvantages to this arrangement.

On the plus side:
(1) Cross-grazing with sheep or cattle is beneficial in that these animals will destroy worm larvae left on the grass by the horses, helping to keep the level of worm infestation down.
(2) They would provide company for a lone horse or pony.
(3) Cattle, particularly, will eat the grasses which horses ignore, encouraging even grazing.
(4) The chances are that an experienced stockman will be keeping an eye on his animals, so that in the event of an accident or illness he might be available to help you out.
(5) The farmer will, in all probability, take the responsibility for maintaining and repairing the fencing around the field, which can prove to be a costly operation.
(6) Last but not least, the rent you pay should be less.

On the minus side, though:
(1) Young cattle, particularly, can make riding in the field very difficult.
(2) You may well disagree with the farmer about the type of fencing used – farmers are very keen on barbed wire (particularly for cattle) and sheep or pig netting which may well be too low or sagging.
(3) Cattle will increase the chances of your horse contracting warbles as they attract the warble fly.
(4) Feeding can be a problem – you will find it difficult and time-consuming to feed your horse with other stock in the field, especially in the winter when you need to put out hay.
(5) You cannot leave any equipment such as jumps or dressage markers in the field as they will be quickly wrecked – even by sheep.
(6) The ground will become badly poached in late autumn and early spring when it tends to be wet, especially a relatively small field.
(7) Finally, check your insurance policy – it can prove extremely expensive, as well as distressing, if your horse should injure or kill stock. Some horses and ponies take a great delight in herding and chasing cattle or sheep, and this behaviour will not endear them to the farmer.

Sharing a field with other horses is not always such a good idea as it might seem. Although an inspection rota can be organised among owners, thus saving time for each individual, the drawbacks often outweigh this advantage.

Feeding is not only difficult but can be dangerous as several horses jostle for the food. Even picking feet out presents a problem as others vie for human attention, and bad habits quickly spread from one horse to another. There is always the risk of injury through fighting, although most horses will settle down and accept a herd leader. Catching your horse when others are milling around can be difficult and frustrating, and it is not usually safe to ride in a field with other horses running free.

On the whole, it is better to try and rent a field where your horse will be the sole occupant for most of the year, and negotiate the loan of some sheep or cattle to cross-graze at specified times. (See Chapter 16.)

Fencing

Check that the fencing is adequate. A good, thick, high hedge is ideal, as it will also provide shelter, but all gaps should be filled with post and rail fencing rather than wire which is difficult for the horse to see. Although a hedge might look impenetrable in summer, any gaps or weak spots will become all too obvious when winter arrives.

Barbed wire fencing should be avoided if at all possible, but if your farmer insists on using it make sure that it is correctly tensioned. If it is loose or sagging a horse can easily get a foot entangled in it and seriously injure itself. It is a good idea to run a single strand of electric fencing along the top of the posts, as once the horse has realised that it is there (and discovered that it 'bites') it will usually steer clear of the fence altogether. It will also stop the horse from leaning over the fence or rubbing against it, loosening the posts.

Normally, a farmer will have no objection to you using this as it will benefit him as well, and if you ask his advice, he may be able to tell you where to get it from and how to use it. Ordinary heavy gauge wire fencing, with two or three strands, is another type much favoured by stock farmers, chiefly because it is relatively cheap. This too must be taut, and will benefit from having a single strand of 'power' along the top.

Sheep or pig netting is also commonly used. The design of its mesh is such that in theory a horse should not be able to get a foot through the bottom rows, but it could easily pull a shoe off – and ponies especially are notorious for proving theories wrong. The safest course is to make sure that the bottom of the fence is at least 12 inches (30 cm) above the ground. The single strand of electric fencing should be run along the top as before, especially since sheep netting is rarely high enough on its own.

Any fence should be at least 3 ft 6 ins – 4 ft 6 ins (106–137 cm) high, or you may find that your equine friend will indulge in some unscheduled jumping practice.

When wire fencing of any kind is used, the top strand must be made clearly visible. This can be done easily by tying strips of brightly coloured plastic (used blue fertiliser bags, cut into strips about 1½ ins (4 cm) wide and the full length of the bag are ideal for this purpose, and any farmer will probably be only too pleased to give you some) at approximately 4 ft (121 cm) intervals along the fence. Knot them securely, and leave the ends (which should be about 6 ins (15 cm) long) trailing. The slightest breeze will keep them moving, and the noise they make will often provide sufficient deterrent.

In recent years, a new type of fencing has been launched which combines practicality with comparatively low cost. This is a fencing 'tape' made from specially strengthened and weatherproofed synthetic material, and can be used in place of wooden rails or wire, or as a top strand to render a wire fence visible. Two types are widely available; electrified and plain, and both have the advantage of being highly visible and totally safe.

The plain type comes in various widths and colours, and is nailed on to ordinary posts. It is maintenance free, and strong enough to withstand a horse running full-tilt into it – but horses will still be inclined to rub and lean, or even chew.

The electrified tape is also available in different widths and colours and is equally strong, but has all the added advantages of electric fencing with none of the drawbacks.

It is secured to normal fencing posts using special insulators, has built-in tensioners and is powered by an ordinary battery or mains 'fencer' unit. It is also possible to buy extended fasteners, which in effect hold the tape away from an existing fence line – a boon where grazing is rented and the farmer insists on using barbed wire. If a single line of tape is fixed in this way, about 9–10 ins (22–25 cm) in front of the top of the existing fence, it will keep the horse away from the potentially dangerous wire.

This electrified tape can also be used effectively for temporary fencing, as in strip-grazing, for example, when only one strand should be needed, but for a permanent boundary fence, two or three 'rails' are recommended.

Post and rail fencing is not so frequently found these days as it is incredibly expensive, but if it is used, check that it is not rotten, and repair where necessary.

The field gate

The gate should be sturdy, sufficiently wide (at least 4 ft – 4 ft 6ins (121–137 cm), should swing easily and be lockable. If the hinges allow the gate to be lifted off them, reverse the top hinge. The gateway should preferably not be in a corner, as this increases the risk of accidents caused by horses or other stock milling about when you are entering or leaving the field.

Water

A clean, fresh water supply is of the utmost importance. The ideal is a trough supplied automatically, although it can be difficult to keep clean.

The best site for any trough is in the open. If it is under a hedge or tree it will quickly get clogged with dead leaves and twigs. An old bath often provides a useful alternative to a trough as it can be emptied regularly, cleaned out and refilled with fresh water.

It is better to allow the level in the trough to fall right down and completely refill it with fresh water than to keep constantly topping up. This will ensure that the trough is regularly cleaned out and the water available to the horse is always relatively fresh.

A useful tip in summer is to leave a plank of wood, covering about two-thirds of the surface area of the trough, floating in the water. This will slow down the rate of evaporation, which in hot weather can be very rapid.

If there is a stagnant pond in the field, it should be fenced off as it is not at all suitable for a horse to drink from, and it is also likely that there will be deep mud at the bottom.

A running stream can provide a good drinking source, with the added benefit that it will not freeze over in winter, but if it has a sandy bottom, beware. Horses will get colic very easily if they take up any sand when they drink.

If you can see no practical way of getting a plentiful supply of water to the field (bear in mind that one horse can drink 5–10 gallons (22–45 litres) a day, and must be allowed to have as much water as it wants) it is worth looking out for a secondhand water bowser at local farm auctions. An advert in the 'Wanted' column of your local paper, or even on local radio, can also produce results, and since a small bowser can be towed behind a car, this can be the answer to your problem.

The mains supply to a self-filling trough must be protected from frost in winter. This can be done by piling well-rotted manure around the end containing the ball-valve assembly and on the ground above the supply pipe. Alternatively a wooden box with a lid can be made to fit around that end of the trough and then filled with insulating material, such as polystyrene foam or loft insulation.

Poisonous plants

You must make sure that the field is free of poisonous plants or trees before the horse or pony arrives – and don't forget to deal with any overhanging branches of yew trees or privet hedges within range of the fence.

One of the most deadly plants (and all too common in some parts of the country) is ragwort. *Every single plant* must be pulled up by hand, roots and all, and burned. If ragwort is found to be growing in an adjacent field, the farmer, by law, is obliged to get rid of it; if, after having been asked to do so he refuses, the Ministry of

Agriculture should be informed. (Don't forget , though, that this applies to you too!)

Ragwort is at its most deadly when it is dead or dying. Unfortunately, it is then that horses are tempted to eat it – normally they will leave it alone when it is growing. Ragwort poisoning causes irreparable liver damage, and symptoms can take months to appear – but by then it is usually too late to save the horse.

Buttercups and aconites, on the other hand, are only dangerous when alive; they are not harmful when dried, as in hay.

Other fairly common plants and trees which should not be accessible to a horse include foxglove, bracken, hemlock, nightshade, laurel, laburnum and ivy.

Normally most horses and ponies will not readily eat poisonous plants unless they are very hungry (with the exception of yew and privet, which ponies, particularly, seem to adore), but it is better to be safe than sorry, and a few hours' weed-pulling is infinitely preferable to watching the suffering and possible death of your horse through your own carelessness.

A great many garden plants are also harmful to horses, the chief offender being grass clippings which quickly ferment and become highly toxic. Unfortunately a lot of people think they are doing a horse a favour by giving it these, and it is often a difficult practice to prevent.

If there are gardens adjacent to your field, you will have to visit each gardener and politely ask him not to throw *anything* over the fence to the horses. If the reasons are tactfully explained, and you also point out that it would encourage them to lean over and demolish anything within range, he should be only to pleased to co-operate.

Shelter

Shade and shelter must be available in some form, even for the hardiest of native ponies. The reasons for this are obvious in winter but it is not always realised that horses can and do suffer from sunstroke in summer.

An improvised field shelter for ponies can be made out of straw bales, well supported and laid out in the shape of a cross. This design will ensure protection from wind and rain from any direction. You must make sure, though, that the arms of the cross are long enough so that if more than one pony is to use it each has sufficient room without jostling, and it must be high enough to provide a worth-while windbreak.

If the land is normally used for agricultural purposes you do not need planning permission for a permanent field shelter, but if you are in any doubt ask your local council.

Further advice on field shelters can be found in the next chapter.

Improvised field shelter made of straw bales

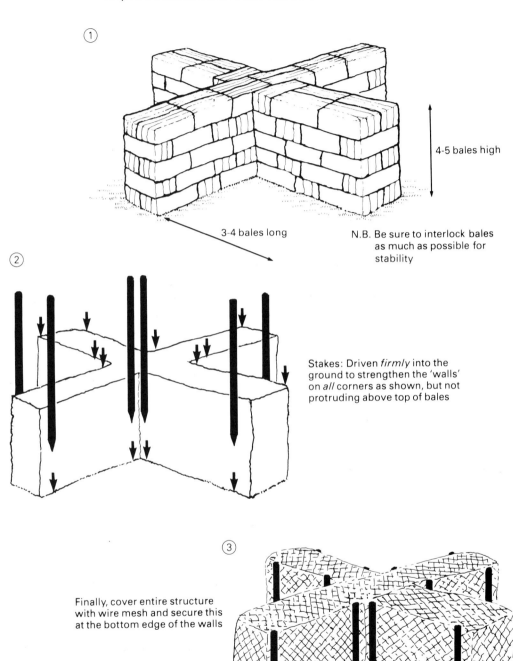

①

4-5 bales high

3-4 bales long

N.B. Be sure to interlock bales as much as possible for stability

②

Stakes: Driven *firmly* into the ground to strengthen the 'walls' on *all* corners as shown, but not protruding above top of bales

③

Finally, cover entire structure with wire mesh and secure this at the bottom edge of the walls

Hidden dangers   If the field is close to houses, or is on a school route, it is a good idea to put a large notice on the gate: *Please Do NOT Feed the Horses/Ponies, IT CAN BE FATAL*. It is amazing what some people will try to feed to horses, either through ignorance – in the case of things like whole apples or carrots – or sheer curiosity, as in 'I wonder if horses like chewing gum?'

A last look round to make sure that there are no dangerous objects in the field; for example bits of scrap, glass or plastic bottles, half-buried wire, rusty nails, etc; and you are ready for the arrival of the horse or pony.

CHAPTER 5

Stables and Shelters

As with grazing, most first-time horse and pony owners are not in a position to pick and choose when it comes to stables, and have to make the best use of any building offered to them, but there are certain basic requirements which must be fulfilled if the horse is to be kept safe and well.

Stable size

Firstly, the stable must be large enough to enable the horse to move around (and turn round) easily. If it is too small the horse will tend to spend most of its time standing still in one place, which will not be good for its legs and feet; it may also bruise its hips or shoulders as it attempts to turn round. Another reason, and probably the most important one, is that it could easily become cast (wedged against a wall so that it cannot get up) when it lies down. Going to the other extreme, it may well refuse to lie down at all, which will also put undue strain on the feet and legs.

If the horse is only to be brought into the stable for grooming etc, or perhaps overnight during severe weather, you might be able to make do with a box of about 10 ft × 12 ft (304 × 365 cm) for a pony or small horse (up to 15.2 hh), but 12 ft × 12 ft (365 cm × 365 cm) would be a better size. A larger horse will require an area of 12 ft × 14 ft (365 × 425 cm) if kept stabled to any great extent.

Long narrow stables, even though they might provide the required floor area, should be avoided since the same risks apply to these as to stables which are too small overall.

There must also be sufficient headroom in order to minimise the risk of the horse throwing its head up and striking it on the roof as this can cause serious injury; horses can also suffer badly from claustrophobia in small, low stables.

The doorway

The doorway must be wide enough so that the horse will not bang its hips as it goes in and out, particularly if it has to turn sharply once out of the door. You must always lead the horse straight through the centre of the doorway rather than expect its body to bend around a 90° turn, and never lead it in or out with stirrups dangling loose from the saddle.

If the horse is to be kept stabled for any reason during the day, the doorway must be high enough so that it can stand comfortably looking out; if it is too low there is again the risk of injury to the head. The overall height of the doorway should be 7 ft 6 ins – 8 ft (228–243 cm), and the bottom half door should be about 4 ft 6 ins (137 cm) high. The actual opening should be 4 ft – 4 ft 6 ins (121–137 cm), and any sharp brick corners rounded off.

Roofing

Many old farm buildings have corrugated iron roofs, which make the stables cold in winter, baking hot in summer and incredibly noisy when it rains. Depending on your tenancy, you could perhaps insulate a tin roof with plaster board or chipboard or consider replacing it with other material.

Secondhand timber for joists to support felt, tiles or slates would be relatively inexpensive, and the job would be well within the capabilities of a DIY hobbyist or local odd job man.

If the stable is only to be used as a short-term shelter for a horse which otherwise lives out, such drastic measures may not be necessary, but you may have to think again if the horse has to be kept confined for any reason.

The floor and drainage

The floor of the stable must be solid, non-slip and have adequate drainage. Again, much will depend on the amount of use the stable will have – and your tenancy agreement – but one of the best, and cheapest, flooring materials is concrete. It should be laid so that it has enough slope to ensure drainage (about 1 in 40), with the slope running from the back to the front. If it slopes the other way, bedding at the back of the stable will tend to get soggy and smelly as the floor will not dry out completely every day. The floor will need to be swilled and brushed clean along the drainage channel every day if the horse is permanently stabled, and every two or three days if the horse is only in overnight.

Drains in the centre of the stable are not good, as they easily become blocked. In all probability the horse will be lying in a soggy wet patch of bedding, and also it is not good for a horse to stand for long periods with its feet at different angles.

The surface of the concrete must be rough so that the horse will not slip, and this can be easily done while the concrete is wet, using a roller or garden rake on the surface. When a concrete floor is laid over a clay or earth floor, 2–4 ins (5–10 cm) of hardcore should be put down first, and a thickness of at least 3 ins (7.5 cm) of concrete laid on top; it is a good idea to reinforce the concrete with lengths of iron, such as old iron bedframes, to minimise the chance of cracking – remember that a horse's considerable weight is pinpointed on very small areas which puts a great strain on a newly laid floor unless adequate foundations are underneath.

You may well find that there is insufficient headroom in an existing building to allow a concrete floor to be laid, and, if this is so, you will have to make the best of whatever flooring is already there.

Clay or beaten earth floors are difficult to manage as they will not drain and can quickly become smelly; obviously such a floor must be thoroughly swept every day, and on no account should a deep litter system be adopted (see Chapter 10). The other major disadvantage is that they are virtually impossible to disinfect thoroughly, as is necessary if a horse has a contagious or infectious disease.

Fixtures and fittings

There should be as few fittings as possible in the stable to minimise the chances of a horse catching itself, a rug or headcollar on a protruding object.

Mangers should be wide and shallow and have no sharp edges; a narrow, deep manger encourages a horse to 'bolt' its food and risks injury to the eyes. Any space underneath the manger must be filled in to reduce the risk of the horse getting trapped when lying down.

Bucket rings – metal loops fixed to the wall in which the water bucket rests – are incredibly dangerous if left empty and a bucket on the floor will do just as well. It should be placed in a corner of the stable near the door where it can easily be checked without disturbing the horse. Thus sited, any spillage is also kept away from the main bed. A horse which habitually knocks buckets over can be foiled by setting them in the centre of an old car tyre.

The bolts on the door must be strong and horse-proof. Never under-estimate the capabilities of an inquisitive or bored horse, so a second latch on the bottom of the door, operated by your foot, is a wise precaution.

Any light switches or power points must be well out of the horse's reach and must be fully weatherproof. The bedding and hay constitute an enormous fire risk, so all electrical wiring must be maintained in first-class condition and concealed behind a metal conduit.

Similarly, any light fittings must be of the outdoor type and also placed well out of reach, ideally protected by bars or a strong wire 'cage'.

Windows must be barred for safety reasons, and the bars should be spaced vertically so that the horse cannot get a hoof between them. Special heavy-duty wire netting – called 'Weldmesh' and obtainable from agricultural or builders' merchants – can be nailed to a frame to cover an otherwise dangerous window.

Under normal circumstances, stable windows rarely need to be opened, since ventilation is provided through the open top door.

Stabled horses are susceptible to draughts, so windows should

THE LIBRARY
BISHOP BURTON COLLEGE
BEVERLEY HU17 8QG
TEL: 0964 550481 Ex: 227

'Sheringham' stable window

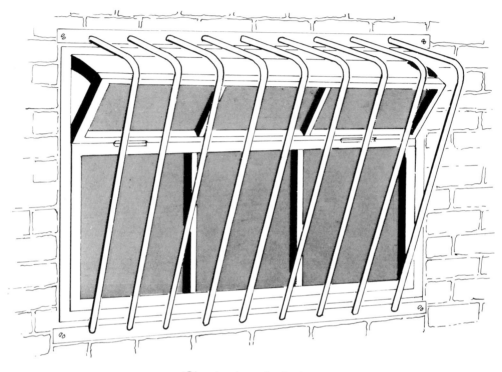

'Sheringham' window
opening inwards, with
protective bars

only open inwards to direct the cold air up and over the horse's back.

The top of the bottom door can be protected by a metal strip to discourage chewing, and any other tempting projections can be painted with a foul-tasting preparation such as 'Cribbox' to serve the same purpose.

The stable must obviously be free of protruding nails, bolts, etc, and holes or cracks in the walls must be patched.

Erecting new stables

If you are thinking of building or erecting new stables, you will have to check first with your local council to see if planning permission is necessary. As a general rule, if the land is a designated agricultural holding, and the stables are not to be erected in the garden, the structure may be exempt – but you will still have to meet building regulations standards.

Wooden stables are becoming increasingly popular due mostly to their price, and the fact that they can, in theory, be taken with you if you move. They tend to be rather hot in summer and cold in winter, though, and if you are considering putting up a new wooden stable, the cheapest is not usually the best. Don't forget to allow for the cost of the concrete base when you are doing your sums – this alone can be almost as expensive as a single stable.

Breeze blocks are a good building material for stable construction. They are comparatively cheap, easy to transport, easy to work with and provide very good insulation against extremes of heat and cold. They must be well weatherproofed, though, as they are porous and frost action particularly will loosen the mortar and crack the blocks.

Field shelters

Some sort of field shelter will be necessary if the horse is to live out and there is no other form of natural shade or shelter in the field – such as trees, hedges, etc. A three-sided shelter can be erected at a reasonable cost using secondhand materials, but make sure that it is large enough to safely accommodate the intended occupants, and that it is sited to give protection from the prevailing winds. Normally, field shelters should be open to the south.

The shelter should not be sited in a hollow, since the ground will quickly become very boggy in winter, and it should not be right in the corner of a field where a horse may feel trapped. Obviously the shelter must be of sound construction and should not leak; like the stable, it must have sufficient headroom.

Horses are notoriously fussy about field shelters and much persuasion may be necessary before your handiwork is occupied. Try putting the hay and feed in it for a while, and feeding nowhere else. If this tactic fails, you may have to put a bar across the entrance and use the shelter as a form of stable – i.e. catch the horse and confine it inside, several nights running, with a good bed of straw and a tempting feed.

CHAPTER 6

Tack and Equipment

The equipment associated with horses and ponies can be divided into three categories: essentials, advisable, and luxury. For the purposes of this book I will not dwell upon the luxuries since there are more than enough items in the first two categories to stretch the average family's resources.

The saddle

For a small child's first pony it is possible to make do with a felt saddle if finances are severely strained, but if at all possible this should be avoided, since not only is it not conducive to a correct – and therefore comfortable – riding position for the child, but also it can make the pony's back extremely sore.

When buying a leather saddle, never ever consider one of the cheap Indian ones, the quality and workmanship of which are truly diabolical. Indian saddles can also do irreparable damage to a horse's back, as not only are the trees normally badly made and inclined to break, but the makers' ideas of the shape of a horse are strange, to say the least.

It is always the safest course to go for a British or German saddle, and these are usually a good buy secondhand.

A point to bear in mind is that secondhand saddles, if properly cared for, will hold their value, and can be regarded almost as an investment, so it makes sense to buy the best you can afford at a sensible price.

When buying a saddle, always have it checked by a professional saddler before you part with the full purchase price. If at all possible, try the saddle on the horse before you buy it, as it is essential that it fits the horse properly. Minor discrepancies in the fit can be made good by a saddler, but the basics must be right.

When placed upon the horse's back, the saddle must sit squarely, with plenty of space between it and the horse's spine along the gullet. The arch and gullet must be wide enough to avoid pinching withers and spine, but not so wide that, when a rider's weight is added, the top makes contact with the horse's spine. The vertebrae of a horse's spine are not designed to bear weight of any kind: the rider's weight is borne by the muscles either side of the spine,

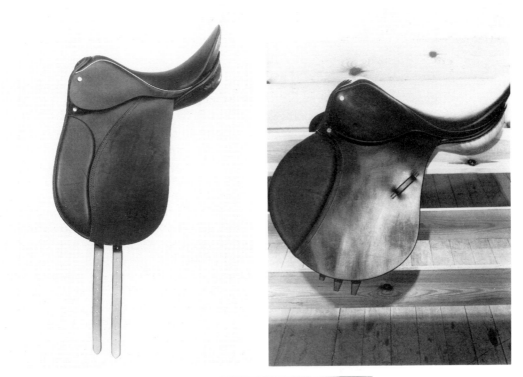

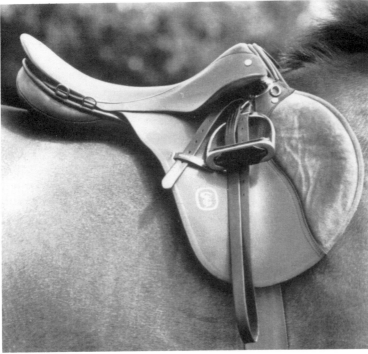

DRESSAGE SADDLE (above left) – note the long, straight, narrow flaps which encourage a longer leg position. The extra-length girth straps allow for closer leg contact with the horse's sides as the girth buckles are below the bottom of the flap.
GENERAL PURPOSE SADDLE (above) – the wider, more forward-cut flaps allow you to ride with short or long stirrups.
JUMPING SADDLE (left) – the short forward-cut flaps are designed for riding with short stirrups.

supported by the ribs underneath. It is important that the saddle does not sit too far back, as pressure is then brought to bear on the sensitive loin region, nor too far forward, which restricts the free movement of the shoulders.

With the rider 'on board' there must be at least three fingers' space between the horse's wither and the underside of the pommel and, leaning forward, the rider must be able to see daylight right along the length of the gullet.

The shape of the saddle should be such that the rider is encouraged to sit in the correct position automatically. If a conscious effort has to be made to achieve this while the horse is standing still, the rider will not have much chance once under way.

The saddle flap should not be so forward cut that it interferes with the horse's movement or forces the rider to shorten the stirrups in order to keep the back of his knee on the saddle. Forward cut saddles are specifically designed for jumping, when the stirrups should be shorter, and straight cut saddles are intended for dressage (or showing in the case of pony saddles) when the rider is aiming for a longer, straighter leg position.

General purpose saddles are shaped in such a way that all the normal disciplines can be carried out relatively comfortably; as such they are perfectly adequate for all but the most dedicated competitors.

Nowadays most saddles are lined with leather, which is comfortable for the horse, easy to keep clean and hard-wearing. Some older saddles were lined with linen or serge, both of which were difficult to clean and tended to wear out. However, using a numnah underneath could save you a lot of work and prolong the life of these linings. (When a numnah is used, it must always be pulled well up into the arch of the saddle before the girths are tightened to ensure that it is not pressing on the horse's spine, and also to maintain a passage of air.)

Spring-tree saddles are more expensive than the rigid-tree type, and are not necessarily better. A good rigid-tree saddle is preferable to a poor spring-tree one, and if a spring tree is used, a numnah must always be worn underneath in order to avoid the horse's spine coming into contact with the saddle when jumping.

The most important point to check when buying any secondhand saddle is that the tree is not broken. A broken tree will do irreparable damage to a horse's back if undetected, and it is an expensive item to replace. Unfortunately the tree can break all too easily if the saddle is dropped on the ground, for example, or if the horse rolls while the saddle is on its back.

Checking the tree for soundness should be left to an experienced saddler, especially in the case of a spring-tree saddle; this test will give you some idea whether or not a rigid-tree is broken: hold the saddle in front of you with the pommel in one hand and the cantle in the other and try to 'twist' it; this should be impossible to do. Then, with the arch against your leg, and the saddle pointing towards you, take the cantle in both hands and try to pull it forward. There should be only a slight amount of give, and any creases appearing in the seat should be straight across at right angles to the gullet.

The leather should be supple and not cracked, and whilst scratches or scuffs will not detract from the strength or performance of the saddle, they will be taken into account if and when you try to re-sell it.

If you are buying a secondhand saddle from a private source, the chances are that it will come complete with girth, stirrup leathers and irons. However, when you consider just how much your personal safety depends on these items, I would recommend that you spend an extra few pounds and buy a new set from a reputable saddler.

Stirrup leathers and irons

Avoid the very thick stirrup leathers made out of cheap 'rawhide', as these will stretch with regular use and are not as strong as their thickness would seem to imply. (They are also very uncomfortable to ride with.)

Stirrup leathers should always be of sufficient length to allow for a good degree of adjustment, but not so long that there is a vast amount of leather trailing.

Stirrup irons should be made of stainless steel; nickel irons are cheaper but are apt to crack, and even break, without warning.

When buying stirrup irons, there should not be more (or less) than ½ in (12 mm) of space either side of the rider's foot when placed on the base of the iron. If the stirrup is too narrow, a foot can get jammed in the iron which could prove disastrous in the event of a fall, and, if it is too wide, the foot can slip right through, with equally horrendous results.

The bar on the saddle which holds the stirrup leather must always be in the 'down' position so that the leather can slide off if the rider is thrown or the iron catches on some obstruction, such as a gate or fence. On some pony saddles the bars do not provide for this, and in these cases safety irons must always be used. These have a large thick 'elastic' band forming the outside of the iron which will come away altogether in the event of a fall.

Girths

Of all the different girths available, nylon string girths probably represent the best value for everyday use. Not only are they cheap to buy but they are also strong, hard-wearing and easy to clean. As they allow free passage of air to the girth region, they are also unlikely to gall an unfit horse, which can often happen with leather girths unless they are kept scrupulously clean and supple.

THE LIBRARY
BISHOP BURTON COLLEGE
BEVERLEY HU17 8QG
TEL: 0964 550481 Ex: 227

Bridles and bits

Your bridle should also be British made, and, again, is often a good buy secondhand. As always check the condition of used leather very carefully, especially where it is folded, e.g. where the bit and reins are attached. If in doubt, have it checked by a saddler.

The bridle must be correctly fitted. If a drop noseband is used, it must not be so low that it interferes with the horse's breathing, so make sure that it rests on the bony part of the nose, and fits snugly below the bit in the curb groove. An ordinary cavesson noseband should be fitted just under the projecting cheekbone, and should not be too tight. The throatlash must have at least four fingers' space between it and the jaw, otherwise when your horse comes down on the bit the throatlash will be far too tight. The browband should be

CORRECTLY FITTED BRIDLE – the drop noseband fits snugly and does not restrict the horse's breathing. The bit is the correct width and height – you can just see the faint wrinkle around the corner of the mouth. The throatlash could possibly be a little tight – allow four fingers' width between throatlash and jaw.

*RUNNING
MARTINGALE IN
USE – you can see that
the martingale does not
interfere with the rein
contact when the horse's
head is in the correct
position, but it will come
into effect if the head is
raised above the angle of
control.*

the correct length – if it is too short, the headpiece of the bridle will pinch the horse's ears, and if it is too long, the headpiece will tend to slip down the horse's neck.

If the reins are too long, they should be shortened. A nasty accident could occur if the rider's foot were to become caught in them.

It may be necessary to use a running martingale if the horse is inclined to throw its head up when excited, but this must be fitted so that it does not interfere with a normal rein contact to the mouth, and only comes into effect if and when the horse raises its head above the angle of control. As a rough guide, the rings, when passed up one side of the neck, should reach to within a hand's breadth of the withers.

Horses which habitually carry their head high are sometimes better with a standing martingale. This is fitted to a cavesson noseband – never to any other kind – and effectively acts on the nose, rather than the mouth. For this reason it is often better to use a standing martingale if the rider is inexperienced, as the rein contact is not affected. Since it will also prevent the horse from stretching its

STANDING MARTINGALE – this does not interfere with the mouth in any way, but must not be too short. With the horse's head in a normal position, you should be able to push the martingale up into the gullet.

neck out, the martingale must not be too tight or the horse will be unable to recover from a stumble, and could well fall. The strap should reach into the gullet with the horse's head in a normal position.

The bit must be of the right width: too narrow and it will pinch and chafe the corners of the mouth; too wide – especially in the case of a jointed snaffle with its nutcracker action – and the bars of the mouth will be bruised when a strong rein contact is taken.

Nickel bits, although cheap, should be avoided. They do not wear well, can suddenly break, and are apt to form sharp edges where the ring meets the mouthpiece.

It is worth noting that a stronger, more severe bit is rarely the answer for a horse which consistently pulls hard; in fact this will normally make matters even worse. If you do experience this problem, seek knowledgeable advice as the solution usually lies in veterinary attention to the teeth or correct schooling.

As a general rule of thumb, the thicker the mouthpiece of the bit, the milder it is, with the very thin bits being the most severe.

When fitting the bridle, the bit should lie in the horse's mouth, on top of the tongue, so that the corners of the lips are only very slightly wrinkled. If placed too high in the mouth it will be most uncomfortable for the horse and could rub raw patches on the lips; if too low it will bang against the teeth and encourage the horse to put its tongue over it, with resulting loss of control.

It is sometimes easy, when re-assembling a bridle after cleaning, to fit the bit upside-down by mistake. As a guide, the centre of the bit should curve towards the front teeth, and not towards the back of the mouth.

Headcollars

Nowadays there are some very good nylon headcollars available. They are inexpensive, strong, hard-wearing, easy to clean, and, as an added bonus, can be obtained in a range of colours which makes them easy to find if they come off in the field. Leather headcollars are much more expensive and require frequent attention to keep them supple, but they do tend to last longer.

As a rule, horses and ponies should not be turned out in a field wearing a headcollar for a variety of reasons, not the least of which is that it makes life very easy for would-be thieves to catch the animals; also they can get caught up on projecting branches etc. However, if you are unlucky enough to have a horse or pony which consistently proves difficult to catch, you may have no alternative.

The headcollar should be fitted so that sufficient room is allowed under the jaw for the horse to open its mouth and chew comfortably; if it is too tight raw patches will appear on the underside of the jawbones; if too loose, the horse could get a foot caught when it scratches its head. The noseband of the headcollar should lie just below the projecting cheekbone, and the throatlash must not be fastened too tightly.

New Zealand rug

A good quality New Zealand rug must be regarded as an essential for the horse's comfort, but since in the long run it will actually save you money on feed bills, it is also an investment.

Care must be taken to see that it fits well, especially if the horse is to live out completely, as an ill-fitting rug will quickly rub raw patches on the skin which can get infected.

It must be long enough from shoulder to tail and shaped to fit the contours of the horse's back allowing plenty of room at the shoulder. As a guide to the right size, measure from the front of the horse's

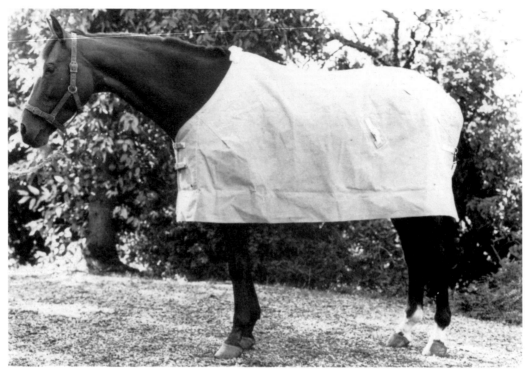

NEW ZEALAND RUG – this is a type which does not require a surcingle to keep it in place. The shaping, crossed leg straps and extra-deep cut will stop it slipping. Note the sheepskin wither pad which helps to prevent rubbing.

chest to the point of buttocks, but always try the rug on the horse before buying.

Some New Zealands have surcingles (which must not be fastened too tightly), while others are extra-deep and the crossed leg straps alone keep the rug in place. Leg straps must be fastened loosely enough to allow freedom of movement, but not so loosely that a foot could get caught when the horse is lying down.

The rug must not be put on a horse which is wet or hot, as the blanket lining will quickly become saturated, and can chill the horse as it cools down; it can also cause a sore back.

The cheapest New Zealands are not, as a rule, the best buy due to their inferior quality, poor shaping and short life. A rug from the middle of the price range would be a better bet and should give many years' wear.

Every couple of years or so, or if the rug starts to leak, it should be re-proofed using one of the preparations readily available from most good saddlers or camping shops. This is an easy, if somewhat messy, DIY job and will help to prolong the life of the rug.

Sweat rug

A sweat rug is another necessity, but should not involve a large outlay. Even in the best regulated circumstances there will come a time when a horse is hot or wet and has to stand in a stable or box to cool down. Sweat rugs work on exactly the same principle as a string

SWEAT RUG – works on the same principle as a string vest, allowing moisture to escape but preventing chilling. This rug fits the horse well, since it covers the loins and is not too deep.

vest, allowing the coat to dry while preventing chilling. When used underneath a stable rug they also provide an amazing amount of extra warmth.

If a horse is very wet or hot and the weather is cold, clean straw can be loosely put under the sweat rug, which will aid the drying process and do away with the necessity for a rug on top until the horse is completely dry – this is known as 'thatching'.

A sweat rug should never be used without a roller or surcingle if the horse is to be left unattended, as it will tend to slip and the horse can easily get a foot entangled in it. For this reason it should never be put on underneath a New Zealand when the horse is turned out.

When buying a sweat rug, check the shape of it, as some makes are not very long in the back, but are extremely deep and this can be dangerous if the horse rolls.

Night rug

Strictly speaking, this need not be an essential if the horse is to live out, but if it is to be stabled overnight in the winter it will need a rug of some kind if a New Zealand has been worn during the day. (The New Zealand will have to be removed to be dried.)

A jute rug – made with a jute outer lined with blanket material – is the cheapest, and would be quite adequate for most horses; if extra warmth is required an ordinary household blanket can be used underneath.

STABLE/NIGHT RUG – made of quilted polyester, is very warm and light in weight. This rug has a surcingle sewn on, but some have crossed straps instead.

The disadvantages of a jute rug are that it cannot easily be washed and it can tear easily.

In recent years quilted nylon/polyester night rugs have come on to the market, and although more expensive they are generally better in that they provide more warmth without weight, are machine-washable and can be dried quickly.

Roller

Jute rollers are quite adequate for everyday use, and can be easily adapted for use when lungeing if side reins are required. The padding either side of the horse's spine should be firm so that the top of the roller does not press on it, and you should make sure that there is sufficient adjustment to allow for various thicknesses of rugs to be comfortably accommodated.

When done up, it should be tight enough to ensure that it will stay in position if the horse lies down or rolls, but not as tight as the girth of a saddle.

Leather rollers will obviously last longer but are much more expensive. In any case, a good quality jute roller should last for the lifetime of a horse.

Lead rope and lunge rein

These should only cost a few pounds, and for safety, should always be bought new. They should both have a swivel-mounted spring clip at one end and a knot or loop at the other.

   When using either, the actual rope must never be wrapped around your hand, as serious injury can result if the horse decides to take off and you are unable to let go. If you are lungeing or leading a horse which you know or suspect to be capable of irrational behaviour, you should always wear gloves to avoid rope burns.

Haynet

Haynets are also cheap, but it is an easy job to make your own from used baler twine, and they can be made to the size you require (see page 38).

Grooming kit
Dandy brush

A brush with long coarse bristles, for use on the body and legs of an unclipped horse in the winter to remove mud, dried sweat, etc. It is too harsh to be used on a clipped horse, and is not recommended for manes or tails as it will break the long hairs. Thin-skinned horses may object if the dandy is used on their summer coat, so don't be too rough with it.

Body brush

This has shorter, finer bristles and is designed to remove scurf etc. from the coat of a clipped horse or for general grooming in the summer. It must not be used on the body of a horse which lives out

GROOMING KIT – a typical grooming kit, showing: in container left to right: dandy brush, stable rubber, body brush; on the ground: exercise bandage, sponge, hoofpick, rubber curry comb, mane comb, curry comb, water brush, hoof oil.

Making a haynet

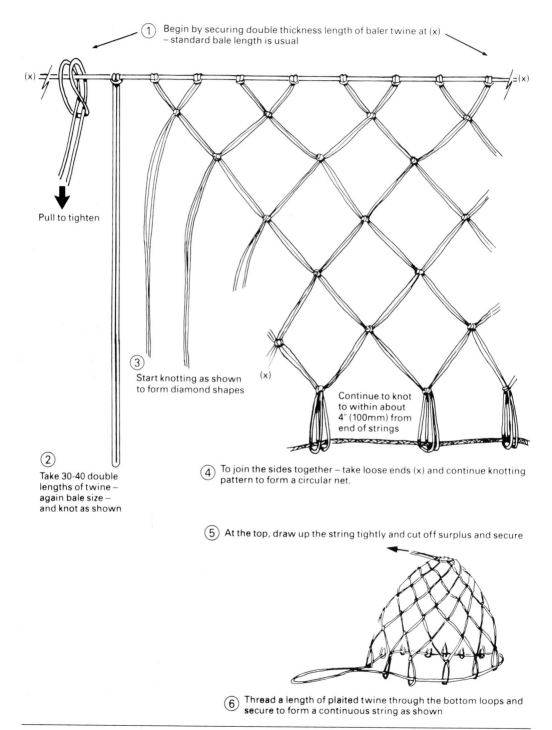

① Begin by securing double thickness length of baler twine at (x) – standard bale length is usual

(x)   = (x)

Pull to tighten

③ Start knotting as shown to form diamond shapes

(x)

Continue to knot to within about 4" (100mm) from end of strings

② Take 30-40 double lengths of twine – again bale size – and knot as shown

④ To join the sides together – take loose ends (x) and continue knotting pattern to form a circular net.

⑤ At the top, draw up the string tightly and cut off surplus and secure

⑥ Thread a length of plaited twine through the bottom loops and secure to form a continuous string as shown

if the weather is at all inclement, as it removes the protective natural grease from the coat. It is always used on the mane and tail.

Curry comb

Used in conjunction with a body brush. It is made of metal and cleans the body brush as you groom. Don't be tempted to use the curry comb on the horse as it is very easy to puncture the skin, particularly over bony areas. After every couple of strokes with the body brush, scrape it across the curry comb and then tap the curry against the wall or on the ground.

A rubber or plastic curry comb can be used on the horse – if it does not object – and is very useful in removing caked mud and loose hair in the spring when the winter coat is being shed.

Water brush

The water brush is long and narrow, with fairly short bristles and is used for washing the horse's feet and laying the mane.

Hoofpick

Buying several hoofpicks is a good idea, as these items have a habit of disappearing. A length of plaited twine or brightly coloured ribbon tied to them will make them easier to locate.

Stable rubber

An old cotton or linen tea-towel makes an excellent stable rubber – for the final finishing touches to the horse's coat to remove any dust.

Sponges

Two sponges are also required, which should be of different sizes or shapes, one for cleaning around the nose and eyes and the other for sponging the dock, sheath (geldings) and udder (mares).

Comb

A mane and tail comb is required for pulling the mane and tail, but should not be used too regularly as it will break the hairs.

Hoof oil

Applied, with a brush, to walls and soles of the feet to help prevent brittleness.

Veterinary equipment

Basic items of veterinary equipment are:

Antibiotic powder and cream

Useful for application to minor wounds and abrasions, though neither should be used if the vet is to attend to stitch a more serious cut.

Purple spray

This is an antibiotic in aerosol form, coloured with gentian violet (hence the name). It is very useful for applications in areas not readily accessible for powder, or where powder or cream would be rubbed off. It is also good for drying wounds which are weeping. The only drawback is that many horses take a rooted dislike to the noise aerosols make, so you have to apply it with care.

Gamgee	This is cotton wool sandwiched between two layers of gauze, and must always be used underneath exercise or stable bandages, and with many other dressings. It comes in a long roll and is cut to size as required.
Cotton wool	Useful for cleaning and swabbing wounds. An economy size roll will last for ages, but keep it in a sealed plastic bag to avoid contamination from bits of hay/straw/other general debris.
Stable bandages	You will need a set of stable bandages made of wool for use over poultices, to protect the legs when travelling and to put on a tired horse. Gamgee must always be used underneath, and the bandage itself must not be too tight.
Exercise bandages	These are made of stretchy material, and are designed to offer support as well as protection when competing or during other strenuous work. Again, Gamgee *must* be used underneath, and although the bandage must be tight enough to support the tendons, it must not be so tight that the circulation is impeded. An exercise bandage can also be used for the tail – and this is the only time it is applied without the obligatory Gamgee. These bandages must be washed frequently in order to retain their elasticity, and should be kept fairly tightly rolled when not in use.
Crêpe bandages	You should always have a couple of wide crêpe bandages on hand. They are used to support an injured limb or can be put over a poultice. Open weave cotton bandages are not suitable as they have no give in them, and do not mould themselves to the contours of the limb.
Poultices	An extremely useful and versatile preparation is Animalintex; this is a ready prepared poultice which can be cut to the desired size, soaked in hot water and applied to a wound. Sold in sealed plastic bags Animalintex can be kept almost indefinitely, and a couple of packets should always be on hand. For more details on their correct use etc. see Chapter 15.
Stockholm tar	This is a delightfully messy, smelly compound used widely in the treatment of foot ailments. It will also keep indefinitely if the tin is well sealed.
Vaseline	This can help prevent cracked heels in horses turned out in wet paddocks. You will also see it liberally smeared over the legs and belly of horses competing in the cross-country phase of one- and three-day events to protect them from knocks and grazes.

Linen	A clean piece of linen, or even a freshly laundered handkerchief, should be kept in a tightly sealed plastic bag for use around the horse's eyes. Cotton wool can shed fibres which will irritate the eye.
Disinfectant	A general disinfectant, such as Savlon or Dettol, will be useful, but it must never be applied to a wound undiluted as it will damage the tissues. In fact, one of the best things to use when cleaning a wound is salt water.
Thermometer	A veterinary thermometer is useful, but be warned: you must keep a firm hold of the end of it when you take the horse's temperature; it is not unknown for it to disappear from view!

Additional items for the veterinary chest

Although not absolutely necessary, the following are nonetheless useful to have in stock:

Negasunt	An antibiotic powder which also deters flies. It is therefore especially useful in the summer months for minor wounds and abrasions.
Protocon	An extremely good (but very expensive) ointment for cracked heels. A cheaper alternative is zinc and castor oil cream, which I find very effective.
Cornucrescine	An ointment used mainly on the coronary band to promote vigorous growth of the hoof, but can also be used on a sore mouth.
A fly repellant	Products such as Extra Tail can be useful for horses which are plagued by flies in the summer. Some preparations are claimed to be longer-lasting than others, and they vary widely in price.
Hydrogen peroxide BP	Very good for cleaning deep wounds in the foot – it should be poured in neat, and as it bubbles up it brings any debris out with it.
Cough mixture	A bottle of Benylin is handy in cases of coughing, and black treacle is also soothing – and can also be used to disguise other medications which have to be given orally.
Epsom salts	These are added to the drinking water of horses on a laxative diet as they have a diuretic effect in keeping the kidneys functioning correctly.
Kaolin poultices	These are useful in cases of sprains or bruising. The kaolin comes in paste form in a tin, which is heated to the required temperature in a pan of boiling water, then smeared on to a pad of Gamgee or cotton wool, and bandaged in place.

Liniment	Liniment, such as is used by sportsmen, can be rubbed in to ease stiff muscles etc., but you must be aware that horses, despite their size, have a much lower pain threshold than humans, so 'human' liniment must be used sparingly.
Methylated spirits	These can be rubbed into the girth area to help prevent galling on an unfit horse; salt water is often just as effective.
Bone radiol	Useful in the treatment of bony enlargements (e.g. splints) but normally your vet will recommend a suitable preparation at the time.
Washing soda and iodine	These are often used in the daily treatment of some skin diseases, such as ringworm and Canadian pox, but nowadays this is backed up by injections and powders given orally. (Washing soda, dissolved in warm water, is also good for removing an accumulation of grease from dirty tack.)
Hardening lotion for legs	An old-fashioned, but effective 'leg brace' (a lotion applied to the lower legs of a horse starting work after a protracted rest) can be made from malt vinegar in which fuller's earth has been dissolved. This should be sponged on the legs before and after exercise each day, and will help to 'harden' the tendons.
Poultice boot	It is useful to make a 'boot' out of strong sacking to go over the foot when a poultice is applied. This will help to make the dressing more secure and the job of bandaging easier.

A WORD OF WARNING	One item which should NOT be in your veterinary kit is a Colic drink or drench as it must *never* be administered by anyone other than a veterinary surgeon. The consequences of the liquid 'going down the wrong way' can, quite literally, be fatal. In any case, nothing should be given to a horse with colic until or unless the vet has seen it, as it can very often make an already serious condition much worse.

Miscellaneous items	There are a number of other pieces of equipment which you will need; some fairly obvious but others less so.
Tack cleaning kit	This should consist of saddle soap or some other preparation which will soften and preserve the leather – note: neatsfoot oil should not be used as it will rot the stitching. Two sponges (one for washing and one for soaping); metal cleaner and a soft cloth.

Feed and water buckets	If a horse has to have a headcollar left on for any reason and it will be eating or drinking from a bucket, you should try to get one whose handle is attached under the rim, as it is otherwise quite easy for the headcollar to get caught on any projecting hooks etc. and this can throw even the most docile of animals into a state of blind panic.
Tools for mucking out	These will consist of a stiff yard broom, a shovel and an agricultural type of fork. If shavings are used for bedding, rather than straw, you will need a specially designed fork to cope with them. A pitchfork is also useful for shaking out fresh straw. Needless to say, none of these items should ever be left in the stable when the horse is in occupation.
A sweat scraper	Useful for removing excess water or sweat from the coat.
An old thick towel	Kept especially for use on the horse, this is a 'must' if the horse is to be given a bath before a show in the summer. Don't forget to use only animal shampoo, as detergent is quite unsuitable for a horse's coat.

Storage

You will need somewhere to keep your feed, hay and straw. Metal feed bins for the storage of hard feed are available from agricultural merchants, some large saddlers and by mail order. They do tend to be expensive, though, and a perfectly adequate substitute is the humble dustbin. The disadvantage with dustbins is that they take up more space than conventional feed bins, but against that they can be moved around freely and are easy to clean. Provided that the lids fit well, the feed should be safe from damp and vermin.

Storage of hay and straw can prove a considerable problem due to their bulk and the fact that they must be protected from the weather. If you have no suitable accommodation, it might be worth asking local farmers if you could rent some space in one of their buildings. This could still work out cheaper than buying by the bale as needed.

Buying some hefty padlocks to secure stable doors and field gates is a wise precaution.

THE LIBRARY
BISHOP BURTON COLLEGE
BEVERLEY HU17 8QG
TEL: 0964 550481 Ex: 227

CHAPTER 7

Choosing and Buying the Right Horse

There is a great deal more to buying a horse than simply deciding what you want and going out to get it. Horses are not machines, and it is not just a question of deciding on a particular type or breed and expecting all such to be the same, although certain similarities of temperament and appearance can be noticed. Each individual horse, though, will be just that – an individual, so not only do you have to be sure of its good health and soundness, but also that its personality matches yours.

Horses are large, powerful creatures with minds of their own, and a difference of opinion between you and the horse could well result in serious injury to either or both of you.

Many first-time owners find themselves 'over-horsed' – an emotive expression which simply means what it says, that the horse is too much for them. This predicament can, to a great extent, be avoided if some careful 'homework' is done beforehand, as can the disappointment arising from a totally unsuitable choice.

Consider first your circumstances. How experienced are you at handling horses? Will you be able to cope with more than a very quiet, safe ride? Will you expect the horse to compete in competitions – dressage, showjumping, cross-country, etc. – and at what level? Do you just want a safe problem-free companion to hack or perhaps hunt? Will the horse be kept stabled or at grass? Will the horse be intended for children or adults?

These are just some of the questions you should ask yourself – each has a part to play in determining the type of horse you should buy. Be realistic – and honest with yourself – and you should avoid most of the major pitfalls.

Points to Consider

Type and breed

You will expect certain standards from your horse, depending on your ambitions. If you are looking for a horse on which to compete at anything higher than riding club level, it should ideally have some Thoroughbred or Arab blood in its ancestry. Half to threequarter-bred, as it is called, would have quite sufficient quality, especially if the other half or quarter were Cleveland Bay, Trakhener or Hanoverian. You would, however, have to be prepared for the horse to show some 'prima donna' characteristics which may not be entirely to your liking.

For a safe, honest horse or pony with which to hack, occasionally hunt or do small riding club competitions, it is worth considering one of Britain's native breeds – Welsh Cobs, Connemara, Fell, Dales, Highland, Irish Draught cross – or a true 'mongrel' with breeding unknown but having the temperament you require.

The exact ancestry of most horses is quite irrelevant unless you want to show it in pure-bred classes – its nature, health, soundness and overall suitability for the job in hand matter far more. For this reason, avoid the flashy good-lookers; their extravagant appearance and behaviour do not often go hand in hand with a calm disposition.

Looks are really unimportant, and indeed some of the best-loved stars of the equine world are quite ugly when seen close to, but their worth is undisputed.

Don't expect miracles. A horse expected to live out all year round and be calm and quiet at all times in all circumstances is unlikely to take you to the Horse of the Year Show or win races – and conversely a potential Olympic three-day eventer cannot be expected to provide a 'bomb-proof' ride for all the family.

Mare or gelding?

Geldings, on the whole, are more consistent than mares; they tend to be less moody and a certain level of performance can be expected from them throughout the year. Mares, however, come into season every three weeks from spring until late autumn, and sometimes during the winter too. Their behaviour at these times can be very erratic; some will become lethargic, others excitable, and a few will show bad temper.

Having said that, the number of mares being used in top-level competition is on the increase. A few years ago, geldings were all the fashion due to their greater reliability, but now it is generally recognised that, with tactful riding, a really good mare can often have the edge since she is more likely to produce flashes of pure genius. For a family, though, a gelding is usually a better bet for all-round dependability.

Age

Unless you have had considerable past experience, don't be tempted to buy a young horse in the belief that you will be able to educate it. Youngsters – up to six or seven years old – require a vast amount of time, patience and expert knowledge.

Whereas good manners seem to take an age to instil, bad habits are picked up at the drop of a hat and literally hundreds of promising young horses have been inadvertently ruined through inexpert handling, becoming a danger to themselves and their hapless owners. Training young horses is much better left to those whose speciality lies in that area.

A horse aged between seven and nine will be old enough to have learned its job, but will still be looking forward to ten or more years of active participation in most riding activities.

The only exceptions are Thoroughbreds who have begun racing as two- and three-year-olds and are subsequently sold into private ownership. As a result of this early strain, they are usually fit only for light hacking after about fifteen or sixteen years of age.

Conformation

The way a horse is put together is called conformation, and before you even look at a prospective purchase, you should be aware of the most common conformation faults and their effect on a horse's performance or suitability.

A kind eye is everything. Avoid a horse which habitually rolls its eyes, showing the whites, as this is a sign of uncertain temperament.

Ewe, or upside-down, neck can prove to be a physical disadvantage as well as being unattractive to look at; the horse will tend to build up muscle along the bottom of the neck rather than the top, and this has not earned the nickname of 'pulling muscle' without good reason.

An upright shoulder increases the chance of injuries caused by concussion, and can make for an uncomfortable ride. Look for a long, sloping shoulder and well-defined withers.

The knee should be broad and flat, giving plenty of room for the tendons and ligaments inside the joint to function freely.

Viewed from the side, the front of the cannon bone should continue in a straight vertical line from the forearm so that the horse's weight is borne correctly; deviations from this are called 'over at the knee' and 'back at the knee'.

The horse must have sufficient 'bone' in relation to its size. The measurement is taken around the cannon and tendon, just below the knee, and this measurement should remain roughly the same from knee to fetlock. A horse with a heavy body and not enough bone is unlikely to stand up to much hard work, and if it is noticeably narrower below the knee than just above the fetlock (called 'tied in at the knee'), again, tendon and ligament problems can arise.

Tendons should be hard, cold and straight. A 'bowed' tendon, one which curves outwards, indicates weakness and is a sign of strain and breakdown. They should also be free from blemish, but, in older horses, bony lumps may be found on the inside of the front legs, just below the knee. These are called 'splints' and are commonly formed as a form of strengthening while the horse is young. The usual cause is too rapid growth or overwork while unfit, and, although unsightly, splints rarely cause trouble in later life provided that free movement is not impaired.

Conformation faults

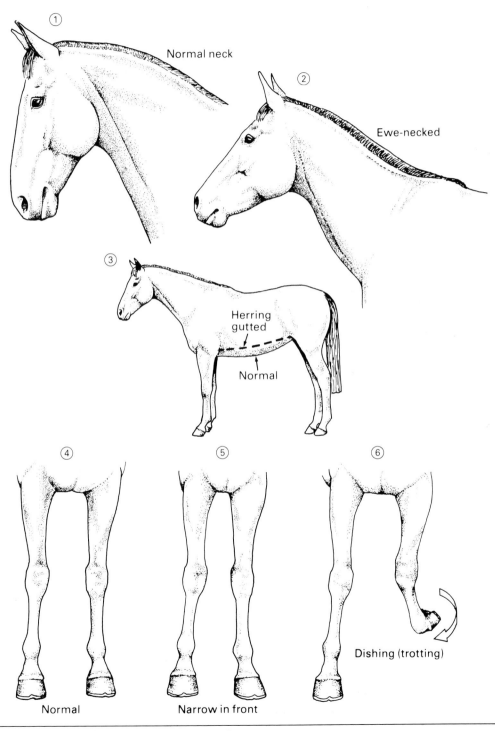

① Normal neck

② Ewe-necked

③ Herring gutted

Normal

④ Normal

⑤ Narrow in front

⑥ Dishing (trotting)

Conformation faults

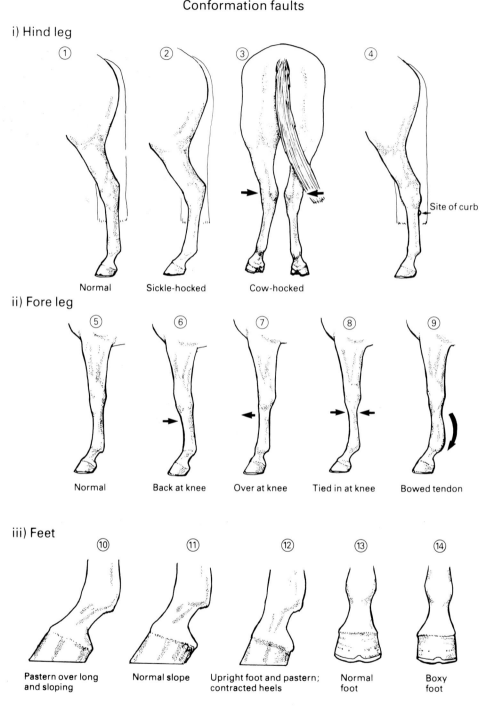

i) Hind leg

1   2   3   4

Normal   Sickle-hocked   Cow-hocked   Site of curb

ii) Fore leg

5   6   7   8   9

Normal   Back at knee   Over at knee   Tied in at knee   Bowed tendon

iii) Feet

10   11   12   13   14

Pastern over long and sloping   Normal slope   Upright foot and pastern; contracted heels   Normal foot   Boxy foot

Points of the horse

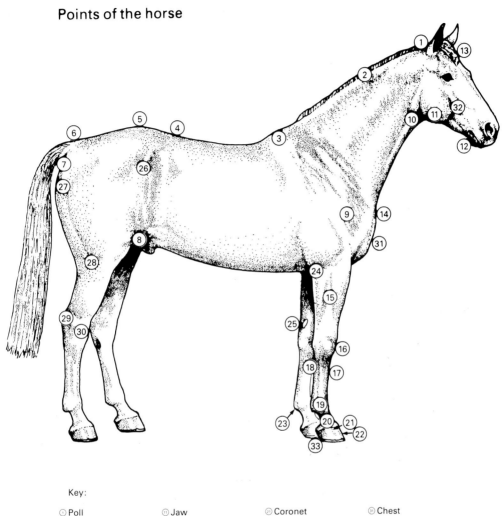

Key:

① Poll	⑪ Jaw	㉑ Coronet	㉛ Chest
② Crest	⑫ Curb groove	㉒ Wall of hoof	㉜ Projecting cheek bone
③ Withers	⑬ Forelock	㉓ Ergot	㉝ Heel
④ Loins	⑭ Point of shoulder	㉔ Elbow	
⑤ Croup	⑮ Forearm	㉕ Chestnut	
⑥ Root of Tail	⑯ Knee	㉖ Point of hip	
⑦ Dock	⑰ Cannon bone	㉗ Point of buttock	
⑧ Stifle	⑱ Tendon	㉘ Second thigh	
⑨ Shoulder	⑲ Fetlock	㉙ Point of hock	
⑩ Gullet	⑳ Pastern	㉚ Hock	

The cannon bone should be fairly short – if very long and thin, it can sometimes prove weak.

The hind legs should be free from blemishes or swelling, with no puffiness around the hock joint or bony lumps below it ('curbs'). The legs should be vertical from hock to fetlock, and not at an angle ('sickle hock'). Viewed from behind, the hocks should not curve towards each other ('cow hock'). When you consider that all the propelling force for the horse's weight – and that of its rider – comes from the hindquarters, the reason for insisting on near-perfect conformation in these areas becomes more apparent.

The pasterns should be sloping and free from lumps. Short, upright pasterns are associated with injuries and diseases caused by concussion as they are one of the main 'shock-absorbers' provided by nature. Any bony lumps are usually a sign of past or future trouble.

The fetlocks should be well-defined; if round and puffy, signs of strain are indicated.

Good feet are of paramount importance; bad faults here will render all other merits worthless. They should be broad, well-shaped and well-matched in terms of shape and size; an odd foot is a sign of something amiss. Boxy feet and contracted heels are undesirable, indicating present or future problems, and the soles of the feet should be concave with the frog prominent. The slope of the feet should be commensurate with the slope of the pasterns, to avoid undue strain.

A horse with a very long back, especially if it is unduly dipped ('sway-back'), often cannot carry a heavy rider, and if it habitually carries its tail to one side, this may be a hint of back trouble already. A short back (called 'roach back' if no dip is apparent) is usually a strong one, and is sometimes the hallmark of a good jumper.

The quarters should be well-muscled and fleshy; the old saying 'a good horse has a head like a duchess and a bottom like a cook' has much to commend it.

When standing in front of the horse, there should be plenty of heart-room between its front legs. A horse which is very narrow in front is said to have 'both legs coming out of one hole' and will often knock one foreleg against the other.

'Herring-gutted' is a term used to describe the horse which has too much 'daylight' between its belly and the ground; the girth should be deep and the ribs well sprung.

Looking from the front as the horse is trotted towards you, its action should be straight. This avoids the risk of one foot striking the opposite leg ('brushing'), or extra strain being put upon the joints if the feet are thrown out to the side ('dishing'), or are crooked on landing.

How to go about buying a horse

The golden rule for all but professional buyers is: never, ever be tempted to buy a horse without knowledgeable advice from a third party who is unconnected with the seller. Although the veterinary inspection will confirm a horse's soundness, it will not reveal whether or not you and the horse are basically suited.

An appealing expression and hasty decision can, in the long run, lead to frustration and heartbreak when the mis-alliance subsequently comes to light, so for your own peace of mind, make sure you are well-advised from the beginning.

Enquiries to local instructors, riding school proprietors, breeders – even the farrier and vet – should put you in touch with someone to help you in search for the right horse. Although you will obviously have to pay for their time, this course will probably save you money in the long run since they will be able to 'weed out' the vaguely suitable from the totally unsuitable either through local knowledge or correct interpretation of advertisements.

There are several ways to go about finding the right horse – some more satisfactory than others.

Word of mouth

This can often be the best route. The reputation of a locally-owned horse is usually well-known – or easily checked – and enquiries made to local vets, farriers, riding instructors, riding club members, Pony Club members, etc., may well yield a suitable animal for sale or loan. (These are also the people to approach when establishing the 'bona fides' of a local horse under consideration.)

Dealers

In the old days, dealers were renowned for their various sharp practices in which a vivid imaginaton played a considerable part, but fortunately their once-legendary 'dirty tricks' are now on the decline.

A reputable dealer cannot afford to endanger his reputation by knowingly selling an unhealthy or unsuitable horse, and a trip to a dealer to view several horses in one place can save both time and money.

Most dealers will agree to take a horse back if it proves completely unsuitable, and although they will probably not refund the full purchase price, it is an option worth bearing in mind. They are also more likely to allow horses to be taken on trial, providing the insurance is in order.

If, however, a dealer tries to talk you into a snap decision without a vet's inspection – another buyer is a common excuse – beware. Be suspicious too if he is reluctant to let you try the horse to your satisfaction.

Sales

Horse sales are frequently held all over the country, and might seem like an obvious target – but my heartfelt advice is: stay away. This is because, for the most part, the only horses to end up in sales are those which, for one reason or another, cannot be sold privately. No caring owner of a sound, healthy horse would willingly subject it to the horrors of the sale ring, knowing that its probable destination is the abattoir.

Apart from 'special' and bloodstock sales, the only regular buyers are the meat traders, and it is truly heartbreaking to see seemingly strong, healthy animals being sold for meat.

It is all to easy to buy one such out of pity, but the chances are that you will regret it later when you discover its shortcomings. By then it is too late, and you will find that you cannot sell it on. Horses bought in this way by private buyers have a habit of turning up at subsequent sales, being passed from pillar to post until they are eventually sold for slaughter. It is in some ways kinder to harden your heart in the first instance and thus play no part in prolonging the horse's misery.

Riding schools

If you have been riding a particular horse at a riding school, you may wish to buy it. This is not always a wise move, as although you would be fully aware of its nature and capabilities, you could well find that it is a different animal when taken away from its familiar environment and companions.

Private advertisements

These can be found in local papers and horsey magazines, and in correct interpretation lies an art – and a suspicious mind.

I am not intending to malign the genuine advertisers and to them I apologise, but, nonetheless, there are very few horses which exactly match the description given by their owners. This is only discovered after a fruitless journey of sometimes many miles.

If, for example, a horse is described as 'not a novice ride', there is a good chance that it behaves like a raving lunatic; 'keen' or 'bold' indicates completely unstoppable; 'unspoiled' or 'untried' is some-times a euphemism for 'can't get near enough to do anything with it'; a 'careful jumper' can mean that it stops dead in its tracks before jumping anything. Again, my apologies to the genuine, but the motto is *caveat emptor* – let the buyer beware.

Trying the horse

Make sure that both you and your adviser ride the horse, and try it at all paces. Jump it if possible and note whether this causes it to become unduly excited. If the opportunity exists to take it on the road, do so, and note its reaction to traffic.

If there are other horses in the vicinity, see if it is bothered by going toward or away from them – a horse which resents leaving others (called napping) is not only extremely annoying, but in certain circumstances can be downright dangerous. It is also an extremely difficult fault to cure.

Take note of the horse's condition. If it is thin and lethargic, it could be that the owner has deliberately cut its feed in order to dampen its usual high spirits; if it is summer and the horse is very fat, its recent diet could well have been grass only – again, it could turn into a completely different animal when corn-fed.

In winter, a fit clipped horse which is quiet and well-behaved without being sluggish is more likely to be genuine.

If the opportunity to take the horse on trial is offered, it is the sign of an owner confident that no hidden faults will emerge. Some perfectly genuine private owners will not allow a horse to go out on trial, since, unless you are known to them, they cannot be absolutely sure of the horse's safety and well-being while in your care.

Before taking any horse on trial, you must check the insurance situation. Never take a horse which is not fully insured, either by the present owner or under a temporary policy arranged by yourself. If there should be an accident, not only will you be faced with potentially enormous vet's bills, but you could also be forced to pay the full purchase price for a horse which could now be incapable of further work – or which may even be dead.

The opportunities available to you while a horse is on trial must not be wasted. Within reason, this is your chance to test the horse in every situation you are likely to meet in the future – always consistent with the animal's safety and your own.

Loading, travelling, shoeing, clipping, traffic, jumping, being caught, behaviour in the stable . . . . the list is long, but careful observation will reveal any quirks of temperament it may have.

Records can be checked, too, for a horse which is supposed to have competed if that is your reason for buying.

Vetting

Before making a firm commitment to buy, the horse must be vetted. This inspection may seem expensive at the time, but is worth every penny since there are numerous conditions which are invisible to the untrained eye but which could well prove serious in the future. You will also find that most insurance companies will insist on a vetting before they will issue a policy – particularly if the horse is considered to be valuable. The vet will determine whether or not the horse is completely sound and free from any blemishes which could affect its performance. He will also check its heart, wind and action before and after a brisk gallop, test its eyesight and verify its age. At an additional cost, X-rays can be taken of the feet and limbs.

CHAPTER 8

Feeding – The Basic Principles

The art of feeding Feeding horses successfully, in order to promote their health and well-being, is more of an art than a science. The secret lies in striking the happy medium between too much food – or of the wrong type – and too little.

In general, it is more dangerous to over-feed than to under-feed. A horse which starts getting too fat must have its food cut down as extra strain is placed on the feet, legs, heart and lungs. If a grossly overweight horse is subjected to sudden violent exercise, the consequences can be severe – and permanent.

You can expect a horse to put on a certain amount of weight after the winter when it has access to spring grass, but if the girth measurement continues to increase and the horse sweats on regular exercise, its rations must be reduced and grazing severely curtailed.

An under-fed horse will tend to be lethargic as well as thin, and some horses are notoriously difficult to fatten successfully.

All horses are individuals, and particularly so when it comes to feeding. Observation, common sense and experience are the key factors in establishing a successful diet, but, as a start, the following guidelines should set you on the right track.

The 'golden rules' (1) *Feed according to age, size, temperament, work done – and to a certain extent, the ability of the rider.*
The age of the horse is relevant in that young horses (up to the age of three or four years) and older horses (over twelve years) will require more food than those in their prime; youngsters because the extra is needed for growth, and older horses to help keep them warm and fight off infection.

The size of the horse can roughly determine the amount of food required when stabled and in work. A very approximate rule of thumb is: if the horse's size is doubled, e.g. 2×16 hh = 32, that is roughly the total food intake per day in lbs. (To convert to kilograms, multiply by 0.45.) If the second figure of the size is doubled, e.g. 2×16 hh = 12 lbs (5.5 kg), that is approximately the amount of hard feed required. The same rule will apply to ponies, but the amounts should be reduced 2–3 lbs (0.9–1.3 kg) of concentrates and 4–6 lbs (1.8–2.2. kg) in total.

The horse's temperament must be considered – there are a great many horses which can work quite satisfactorily on little or no hard feed from spring through until late autumn, but which become almost uncontrollable when fed oats. If this is the case, and the horse does not lose weight or condition when worked, then there is no reason why it should have hard feed as a matter of course – think yourself lucky that your feed bills will be low.

Horses expected to do any amount of hard, fast work will require more hard feed and less bulk as they will need more energy than those kept purely for hacking. If the horse is to be ridden only three or four times a week on fairly gentle exercise, and is otherwise out at grass, you will probably find that no additional feeding is required in the spring and summer, and only a small amount, in addition to good hay, is needed during the autumn and winter.

The ability of the rider also has to be taken into consideration; there is no point in having a horse so 'corned up' that its rider, if relatively inexperienced, cannot control it. There are several non-heating compound foods on the market which fit the bill admirably in these circumstances, and the manufacturers' recommendations should be followed.

Oats are still the primary source of energy, but if the horse's behaviour is adversely affected, look to other energy-giving foods. (See 'Notes on feedstuffs'.)

(2) Feed little and often.
In its natural state, the horse's stomach will nearly always be two-thirds full when out at grass, and it is for this reason that hard feed and hay should be given to the stabled horse in 'instalments' throughout the day, rather than in one fell swoop.

The hard feed ration should be divided into at least three, and preferably four, portions, with the amount in each feed being gradually increased through the day, so that the largest feed is given last thing at night.

Apart from being more beneficial to the digestive system, this will also help to stave off boredom, which is the chief enemy of the stabled horse.

(3) Water before feed.
Fresh clean water must be available to horses twenty-four hours a day, as they will drink 5–10 gallons (22–45 litres) a day. If, however, the horse is due for a feed after water has been withheld for any reason, it should be watered first. Large quantities of water drunk immediately after a feed will 'wash' much of the feed through the system losing nutritional value in the process.

Water given to a hot, tired horse must have the chill taken off, as ice cold water drunk while in this state can cause colic. In any event water must not be given to a horse which is still blowing hard after exertion.

Water should be taken away two hours before any hard, fast work, such as a cross-country round, as the horse's performance will otherwise suffer.

(4) *Don't feed before work or when exhausted.*

When a horse is worked, digestion is halted, as blood needed to aid digestion is diverted instead to the lungs so that they may cope better with the extra exertion. Since food is retained in the horse's stomach for an average of one to one and a half hours, hay and hard feed should be withheld for at least this amount of time before any hard or fast work.

Similarly, you should not give a large feed to a very tired horse until it has had at least an hour to recover, as it will be unable to digest it properly. A small amount only may be offered as a 'reward', after a small drink of water.

(5) *Clean utensils.*

Mangers and any utensils, such as scoops or buckets, must be kept scrupulously clean. Apart from the obvious dangers of contamination from stale or fermented food, horses are notoriously fussy feeders, and will often refuse to eat from a bucket or manger which contains traces of a previous feed.

(6) *Vary the diet but don't make sudden changes.*

Some horses are like people, they become bored with the same, unchanging diet every day. Although the basic requirements will remain constant, you can introduce different foods of the same type from time to time to retain the horse's interest.

Any changes in the diet must be introduced gradually over a period of several days, since the bacteria in the horse's intestine can only cope with certain foods at any particular time. As a new food is introduced, different bacteria are produced to deal with it so, if a large quantity of a totally different food is eaten, it will not be properly digested.

This is one reason why a previously stabled horse must not be turned straight out to grass; it must be turned out for a gradually increasing length of time each day, beginning with just an hour or so, in order that its system may adapt to the new diet. After a week or ten days, the changeover will be complete and the horse can be turned out altogether.

(7) *Feed only the best quality food.*
(See also 'Notes on feedstuffs.)
Musty, dusty or mouldy feed must be avoided at all costs. Possibly the horse might in any case refuse to eat it, but it carries the risk of colic or permanent respiratory damage. Hay, particularly, must be of top quality.

Grain, such as oats or barley, must also be clean, sweet-smelling and free from dust, and will start to lose feed value after six to eight weeks, becoming stale if kept any longer. Most horse cubes keep well, but they will not stay fresh indefinitely and should be thrown away if they start to crumble.

Feedstuffs bought from a merchant, and not up to standard, should be the subject of strong complaint – only in this way will action be taken to improve the quality.

(8) *Plenty of bulk.*
The horse has a very small stomach in relation to its size, but a large capacity intestine, and it is essential that it eats plenty of fibrous bulk in proportion to the concentrated food. Hay, particularly meadow hay, is the prime source of this bulk, and chaff (chopped hay or oat straw) or bran should be added to each hard feed as well.

Spring grass is often too rich for many horses, and it may prove necessary to curtail the grazing of horses and ponies which are prone to laminitis (fever of the feet – one cause of which is too much protein). They should be brought in during the day, and given small amounts of meadow hay at regular intervals. They can be turned out overnight so they derive some benefit from the new grass.

(9) *Feed at regular times.*
Stabled horses, in particular, are creatures of routine; they come to expect certain things at certain times and can become quite bad-tempered if kept waiting. Quite apart from this, they should not be left for more than four or five hours between feeds during the day, as this can prove detrimental to the digestive system. A regular routine should be established, and adhered to if at all possible.

(10) *Feed something succulent every day.*
Stabled horses are often very fussy feeders, and it can be quite difficult to find something to tempt them with. Sliced carrots, quartered apples or even freshly pulled grass can be added to their hard feed to stimulate their appetite and retain their interest. Don't be surprised if your horse carefully picks out all the succulent bits and leaves the rest. Even though the horse may pick and choose during the day, you will normally find that it will clean up its feed overnight. If, however, it refuses to eat anything for more than twenty-four hours, veterinary advice should be sought.

(11) Dampen all feed.

All hard feed, with the exception of cubes, must be damped before feeding. Very little water is needed, but the feed must be thoroughly mixed as horses can easily choke on dry food or even inhale it.

Horses with respiratory problems will need to have their hay damped also; this is best done by filling a haynet with the required amount, then tying it to a fence or wall and dousing it with one or two buckets of water. Allow the excess to drain off, and it can then be given to the horse.

In winter months soaked sugar beet pulp may be used in place of water to mix in the feed (see 'Notes on feedstuffs').

Notes on feedstuffs

Hay

Good hay is the basis of all feeding – whether the horse is stabled or grass-kept – and the quality is of utmost importance. Dusty or mouldy hay must on no account be fed, as the spores from this will swell in and obstruct the moist respiratory passages, ultimately damaging the lungs.

Good meadow hay, cut from permanent pasture, provides a wide range of herbs and grasses and is quite adequate for the majority of horses. It is soft, sweet-smelling, highly palatable and forms a vital part of a laxative diet as it is easy to digest.

Horses in hard, fast work are normally fed seed hay – cut in the first or second year from rye grass sown especially for this purpose – and which contains much more protein. It is quite hard and stemmy, and should be light golden in colour.

Hay which has been left out in the sun for too long will become 'mowburnt', when it will be brown, dry and brittle; hay which has been baled wet, in addition to smelling sour and ultimately becoming musty, will also tend to heat in the stack. If unnoticed, this heat will build up until the bales catch fire; for this reason it is a good idea to leave a passage of air between bales when stacking them, and feel the inside of the bales from time to time. This precaution should be taken even if the new hay is thought to be dry, and at the first sign of heat, remove the bales from any building and spread them out in the hope of fine weather to dry them out.

Bran

Years ago, nearly all stabled horses were fed bulk-providing bran, along with oats, at every feed – and in addition had a weekly bran mash as a matter of routine. Nowadays equine nutritionists do not recommend this practice, since in recent years evidence has emerged to show that bran, when fed to excess, can cause calcium deficiency in some horses.

However, it still remains a good way of preventing the build-up of protein in the blood of horses off work but kept stabled, and forms an essential part of a laxative diet. It must be fed in moderation, though, i.e. no more than 2–3 lbs (0.6–1.3 kg) a day.

To make a bran mash: put 1½–2 lbs (0.6–0.9 kg) bran, 1 teaspoon of salt, and a handful of oats or other grain into a bucket; add boiling water, mixing well, until the mixture is crumbly but not sodden. Cover the bucket with a towel and leave to cool. After about 10–15 minutes, test the temperature and feed when the mash is comfortably warm to your hand. A fussy feeder can often be tempted by adding a few sliced carrots (cut into thin fingers) or an apple cut into quarters.

Any horse due to be laid off work or turned out to grass must have its hard food cut down three or four days beforehand, and bran mashes given at night. Bran mashes (and no grain) must in any case be given immediately to a stabled horse whose work is suddenly suspended – for example, due to accident or illness.

Chaff

Instead of bran, chaff can be fed to add the necessary bulk and roughage to the hard feed. Home-cut chaff – chopped oat straw or good hay – is by far the cheapest option, once a secondhand chaff cutter has been purchased or borrowed. Failing this, chaff can be bought by the bag, or a branded product – such as Mollichaff – used instead. Minerals and vitamins, together with molasses, are usually added to the branded products, and they will often tempt a difficult feeder.

A handful or two of plain chaff, mixed in with the feed and damped, will also make the horse chew the food properly.

Oats

Oats are the primary source of energy, and have been a traditional food for horses for many years. Oats should be fed rolled, crushed or bruised; whole oats tend to go straight through the system unless boiled first. Feeding too many oats will make most horses extremely high-spirited, and, in some cases, uncontrollable.

Barley

Barley can be fed crushed, rolled or flaked (pre-cooked). Whole barley must be boiled, but is an excellent fattener. Barley has the advantage over oats in that it provides energy without adversely affecting the horse's behaviour, but can cause heat 'bumps' and/or filled legs in some horses. For this reason it is usual to substitute barley for only part – rather than all – of the oat ration. It is, however, an excellent addition to the feed of horses living out in the winter when the food they eat is being used primarily to keep warm.

Flaked maize

Flaked maize is another good fattening food; again, it can be 'heating', but, if fed along with oats, will supply energy and condition.

Horse cubes

Horse and pony cubes (commonly called nuts) contain a mixture of grain, cereals, dried grass meal, vitamins and minerals, and are a useful feed for animals which hot up if fed oats. There are numerous types, varying from maintenance cubes – for horses doing little or no work – to competition and stud cubes which have the highest protein levels.

'Complete' nuts provide a good balanced feed in themselves when fed with hay, and mean that feeding can be safely left in other, perhaps less capable, hands if you go away. It is more usual, however, to feed nuts along with oats and barley as the hard feed ration, since in this way you can make variations in the diet to prevent the horse becoming bored and perhaps even refusing to eat at all.

Coarse mix

Coarse mix also provides a complete hard feed and comes in various types to cater for all needs. It is a good way to begin feeding a new horse, especially if you are unsure of the correct balance of individual ingredients. Care must be taken not to overfeed as the manufacturers' recommended amounts tend to err on the generous side. Although coarse mix contains all the necessary constituents of a balanced diet and eliminates the guesswork, it does tend to work out quite expensive.

Sugar beet

Pulped sugar beet, in the form of shreds or cubes, is another useful addition to the diet of grass-kept horses in winter. Containing a high proportion of easily digested sucrose, it is a bulk- as well as warmth-provider, but should not be fed to excess – no more than about ½ lb (0.25 kg) dry weight per day.

It must be *well soaked* before use, as the pulp will otherwise swell in the stomach and can cause colic or choking. Soak the pulp in at least double its volume of water, leave for 12 hours and feed within the following 24 hours, mixed in with the rest of the hard feed.

Salt

Salt is a much under-rated part of the horse's diet. The correct functioning of the kidneys depends on the amount of water drunk, and salt plays a vital part in ensuring that the water intake is sufficient.

Vitamins and minerals

A solid lick or block in the stable will serve two purposes. Apart from providing the necessary vitamins and minerals which may otherwise be lacking in the diet, it will also give the horse something to do and help to alleviate boredom. Grass-kept horses are better with a supplement incorporated in a small feed, and your vet will advise on the type required.

Pick-me-ups

Milk (fresh or dried), raw eggs (only occasionally) and beer or stout are often well-received by horses in hard work when mixed with their feed. They are also good to tempt a fussy feeder, or a horse convalescing after an illness.

THE LIBRARY
BISHOP BURTON COLLEGE
BEVERLEY HU17 8QG
TEL: 0964 550481 Ex: 227

CHAPTER 9

Grooming

Grooming, apart from cleaning the coat, helps to stimulate the blood circulation under the skin and is also a good opportunity to look for scratches, scrapes or other minor wounds which may have escaped detection.

Grooming the grass-kept horse

A horse which lives out should not be thoroughly groomed, except during mild weather in the summer; a quick brush over with a dandy brush to remove mud etc. from the areas in direct contact with the tack, any 'foreign bodies' or tangles removed from the mane and tail with the body brush and the feet picked out are all that is necessary before you can ride in the winter.

If you are unfortunate enough to have a horse living out on clay soil you will probably find that thick mud of this nature is almost impossible to remove from the coat. A rubber or plastic curry comb will be more effective than a dandy brush, but care must be taken when going over bony areas such as the knees, withers, hocks and hips, as it is easy to cause bruising if you are a little over-enthusiastic.

In summer the body brush can be used on the coat, and will make it shine. A dampened stable rubber (or tea-towel) lightly wiped over the body as a finishing touch will remove all traces of dust.

Grooming the stabled horse

A stabled horse will require a more thorough grooming programme. In winter when it is clipped the constant wearing of rugs will tend to make the coat dull and lifeless, so in addition to the normal brushing with the body brush every day, it should be 'strapped'.

In the old days this was always done with a wisp of hay, but nowadays 'banging pads' (round or oval leather pads stuffed with horsehair) are often used instead. The object of strapping is to tone the muscles and promote increased blood supply and circulation to the skin. For this reason it should be carried out after exercise when the horse is warm and the pores of the skin are open.

Starting with the side of the neck, raise your arm and 'bang' the muscle with the wisp or pad, in the direction of the coat, as hard as the horse will tolerate. (You may find that some horses will take a while to get used to this strange behaviour, and will be convinced that you are trying to punish them; if you start gradually and just bang gently to begin with, talking soothingly while you do so, the horse will learn to relax and enjoy it.)

You should start with possibly five or six 'bangs' on each spot, building up to fifteen or twenty after a couple of weeks. The only places to strap are: each side of the neck, along the top muscle; the shoulder muscles; the top of the quarters and the thigh muscle.

You should always tie a horse up while you are grooming. Apart from making life easier for you it will also teach it to stand still while you strap.

In theory you should bang in time to the heartbeat; in practice one bang every 2–2½ seconds, keeping a rhythm, is about right. Once the rhythm is established, you will see the muscle you are banging will contract just before the next blow is due to fall, and then relax. It is precisely this contraction and relaxation of the muscles which will tone and harden them.

The correct routine for a stabled horse is to 'quarter' before exercise. Firstly, the front fastening of the rug should be undone and the rug pulled back over the roller while each side of the neck is brushed; the front of the rug is then replaced and the back thrown forward to expose the loins and hindquarters which are also brushed each side. Any stains can be washed off with water, and dried with a towel. The rug is finally put back in position and the horse then given its first feed.

The object of quartering is simply to make the horse look presentable when taken out on exercise. Upon return, it should then be thoroughly groomed and strapped before being rugged up and given its midday feed.

The feet of a stabled horse should be oiled (with hoof oil) every day, as they will tend to be more dry and brittle than those of a grass-kept horse; remember to oil the sole and frog as well as the wall.

Care of the mane and tail

The mane and tail will require trimming from time to time, and while scissors can be used to trim the end of a horse's tail, they must never be used on the mane. The mane should only be shortened by 'pulling': if cut with scissors, no matter how carefully, it will look thick, 'lumpy' and uneven.

To pull a mane begin by giving it a thorough brush with a body brush then comb it carefully with a mane comb. If necessary, stand on something to enable you to reach comfortably (a plastic milk crate is ideal).

If the horse is likely to fidget after a while, it is better to start at the poll because it is in this area that any movement of the head will have the greatest effect on your handiwork – and your temper.

Take a few hairs at a time (about 1 in (25 mm) wide section),

*PULLING THE
MANE – 'back-
combing' the upper
hairs. Only pull a very
few hairs from the
underside of the mane at
a time, with a quick
downward tug.*

comb them down while holding the ends between your fingers, back-comb until you are left holding only perhaps six or a dozen individual hairs, then pull these out with a quick downward tug. Taking and pulling the longest hairs from the underside of the mane each time, work your way along the mane until it is level. If it is still too long, start at the poll again and work your way along, but make sure that the hairs actually pulled out are those from the underside of the mane rather than those whose roots are on the top, or far side, of the crest.

If a lot of pulling is required to achieve the desired effect, it should be spread over a period of several days, or the crest could become reddened and sore.

If a mane is really long, and the length needs to be drastically reduced, you can cut *some* of it off with scissors – but only a length which subsequently needs to be shortened by at least 2½–3 ins (62–75 mm). In this way all the cut ends will be pulled out, and the horse is spared the possible discomfort of extensive pulling.

It is much better to pull a small amount regularly, before the mane gets too long, than to leave it for months on end and have a monumental task to make it look presentable.

Pulling can often be very hard on the fingers and the wearing of gloves is not always practicable as you tend to lose too much 'feel'.

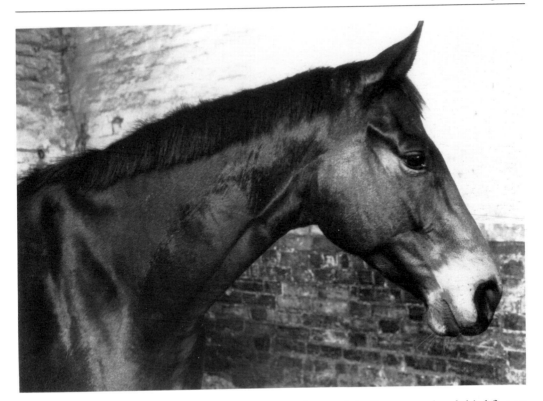

A PULLED MANE – this mane has been pulled to a length suitable for plaiting, and is very neat and even.

Strips of Sellotape wrapped around the first, second and third fingers of the hand with which you actually pull will ease the situation considerably.

Certain native breeds, and many cross-breeds, will tend to have very thick manes of coarse hair which will resist all your attempts to make them lie flat and look tidy. These are best left fairly long (7–9 ins/177–228 mm) and natural looking. If pulled much shorter they will simply stand straight up on end, or, as sometimes happens, stand up in some places and lie flat in others – which looks even worse.

If the mane is fine hair, or you will be plaiting it regularly, you can pull it to a length of 3–4 ins (76–101 mm). Damp it with a water brush every day to help keep it flat, or damp it and put into 'bunches' with elastic bands every 2 ins (50 mm) or so.

Pulling will thin as well as shorten the mane, so if the mane is already thin enough but not sufficiently short, you can break off the ends of the hairs to the desired length – again, they should not be cut with scissors.

'Hogging' the mane (taking it right off with clippers) should not be done except as a last resort for a cob-type pony with a very thick neck as a hogged mane will never grow out properly if you should change your mind in the future.

The horse's tail may also require pulling if it is very bushy at the top, but to do so will put you in a very vulnerable position if the horse objects.

After brushing thoroughly, pull just a few hairs at a time from alternate sides of the tail starting at the root and working down for only 4–5 ins (101–127 mm). The hairs must be pulled from the sides of the tail, and not the top, or unsightly bald patches will result. Make sure that the tail looks 'even' on both sides and, again, don't be too enthusiastic or the horse will probably rub itself raw as soon as your back is turned.

There are advantages and disadvantages in pulling the tail: a pulled tail will require frequent bandaging in order to keep its appearance neat, but will look smart enough for 'special occasions' without any additional attention, whereas a tail left to grow naturally may have to be plaited – a dying art – for shows etc., but can otherwise be left to its own devices.

A happy medium is the usual solution – a tail pulled just enough to avoid the bushy look, but not so much that it requires bandaging every night in order to look presentable.

The bottom of the tail should not be cut without allowing for the way in which the horse normally carries it, i.e. slightly raised. It is usual to cut the tail straight across so that it reaches to about 3–4 ins (76–101 mm) below the hocks when carried normally. You can allow for this by placing one hand under the root of the tail and lifting it slightly before cutting it. A tail which is too short will look ridiculous and also prevent its effective use in warding off flies in summer.

Bathing

In the summer months, a grass-kept horse will need a little more than ordinary grooming in order to look its best for shows or other special occasions, as even a regularly groomed summer coat will be very dusty.

Provided that the weather is mild, a bath the night before a show will work wonders, and it is a simple operation to carry out.

You will need a bucket of warm water to which a proprietary brand of animal shampoo has been added (do not use detergent, such as washing-up liquid or washing powder), a fairly large and soft sponge, a sweat scraper and a thick towel. Washing soda can be added to very hard water as it will help to remove grease from the coat and also make the shampoo more effective.

The soapy water should be sponged all over the horse, starting with the mane and head, taking care that the water does not run down into the horse's eyes, then continue soaping over the rest of the body and legs, finishing by holding the bucket up to the horse's bottom and immersing the tail in the water.

Surplus soap and water is then removed with the sweat scraper, by bringing it across the coat in a downwards direction and finishing off by passing it along the belly.

With another bucket of plain warm water and a clean sponge, thoroughly rinse the horse all over, again finishing with the tail which is immersed in the water and gently agitated to remove the soap.

Remove as much water as possible with the sweat scraper, then give the horse a good rub with the towel. Take the tail hair in one hand, just below the end of the tail bone, and swing it vigorously to spin off the excess water. A tail bandage should then be applied, taking care that it is not too tight. (It has been known for a tight tail bandage, left for several hours unchecked, to cut off the blood supply to the tail.)

Comb the mane and lay it flat. If it is not to be plaited the next day, dividing it into sections and putting it in 'bunches' should ensure that it will lie flat when dry.

After a bath put a sweat rug on the horse and walk it round in the sun until dry. If it has to stand in a stable, make sure there is a good bed of clean straw as many horses will want to roll when turned loose.

Once dry, a cotton rug (or summer sheet as it is often called) should be put on for the night.

Plaiting

As a general guide, the horse's mane should be plaited for: affiliated showjumping, dressage (affiliated and unaffiliated), showing, one- and three-day events (except during the cross-country phase when it is more usual to leave the mane loose) and hunting, when it is done as a mark of courtesy to the Master. It is not necessary to plait for hunter trials, unaffiliated showjumping or gymkhanas (except in best turned out or working hunter pony classes).

Certain breed classes for show horses and ponies, such as Arabs, Mountain and Moorland, stipulate that the mane is left loose.

Tails which have been allowed to grow naturally should be plaited for show classes, but apart from these it is really a matter of personal choice whether you plait the tail or not.

Plaiting will usually enhance the overall appearance of most horses, so if this is an important consideration for any reason, the mane should be plaited as a matter of course.

Plaiting the mane

To plait the mane you will need: a water brush to wet the mane, a mane comb (preferably a small one with fairly fine teeth), a pair of scissors, strong thread of the same colour as the mane, a darning needle and some elastic bands or hair clips. As with pulling the mane, standing on a milk crate may make the job easier.

Elastic bands can be used instead of thread to secure the plaits, and if the plaits are not expected to stay in place for long, they are quite adequate. However, sewing is more secure.

First, wet the mane thoroughly, and comb it flat. Divide it into

PLAITING THE MANE (1) – the next section of hair is kept out of the way with a hairdressers' grip while the first is plaited.

PLAITING THE MANE (2) – securing the end of the plait, which is nice and tight.

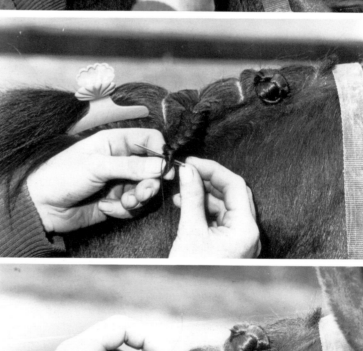

PLAITING THE MANE (3) – having rolled up the plait, it is sewn in place. The completed plait on the right shows the finished product.

sections 2–2½ ins (50–62 mm) wide, depending on the thickness of the mane, and count them.

In the old days, hunters would have seven or nine plaits up the neck, plus one for the forelock, but nowadays most people tend to have more. A short necked horse looks better with a lot of small plaits; a long necked horse with fewer. There should still be an odd number up the neck, though, otherwise the horse's neck will look as if it has been divided in half.

You will find it easier if you secure all the sections with elastic bands or large hair grips before you start plaiting. Also, thread the needle with a suitable length of thread – no longer than 18 ins (45 cm) or so – with a good knot at the end, and keep it within easy reach, but not where the horse could get hold of it.

Starting at the poll, divide the first section into three equal portions, and plait them tightly to the bottom. Secure the bottom of the plait by pulling the thread through the middle of the plait and then taking it once round either side of the knot. Keeping hold of the needle, roll up the plait, with the end underneath and keeping it flat, until you have a neatly folded roll about 1 in (25 mm) long, which will lie flat against the horse's neck.

Bring the needle through the middle of this, through all thicknesses and take it once round either side of the plait, passing through the loop of thread in the centre each time. A couple of passes backwards and forwards through the centre, finishing underneath, and the thread can be cut off. The plait will be secure, and there will not be an unsightly mass of sewing visible.

Continue down the neck, making sure each section is wet before you plait it, and put in one plait for the forelock. If the mane has been pulled evenly, all the plaits will be the same size.

Don't be dismayed if your first few efforts are less than perfect. It takes practice to master the technique, and a lot will depend on the type and length of the mane.

Allow yourelf plenty of time for this operation – anything from half an hour upwards. Properly sewn plaits should stay in place overnight if the horse is stabled, and it makes sense to tackle the plaiting the night before a show when time is not so critical. If necessary you can repair one or two plaits the next morning, but at least you should not be faced with having to do them all when time may be short.

Plaiting the tail

The object is to take hair from the sides of the tail and incorporate them into a central plait which runs down the length of the tail bone.

A pulled tail cannot, of course, be plaited successfully as the hairs of the sides of the tail are not long enough; a tail bandage put on after the tail has been washed will be sufficient to make it look neat and tidy for a show.

A natural tail should be plaited as follows:

Damp the top and sides of the tail and comb through; make sure that your needle is threaded and easily accessible. Starting at the very top, take a section of hair (about ½–¾ in/12–18 mm wide) from each side of the tail in each hand, and draw them to the centre. Pick up a third section (of corresponding thickness) from the middle and start the plait. To create a smart, raised plait, pass each outside section *under*, rather than over the plait as you would normally do, and keep the plaiting tight.

Continue down the tail, taking hairs from each side and plaiting

PLAITING THE TAIL – the first part of the plait completed, the central section only is then plaited to the end of the hair, then looped underneath and stitched in place.

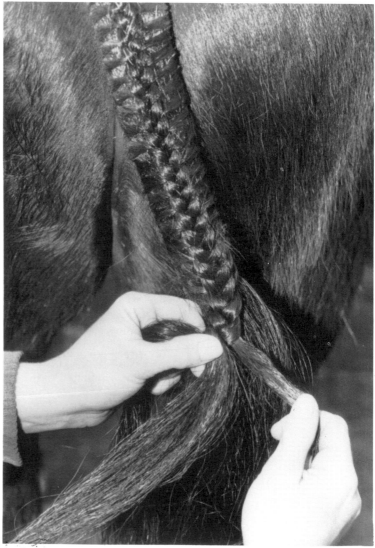

LISBURN
DIVISIONAL COLLEGE
LISBURN HOLTDALE SITE
TELEPHONE 608631 Ex. 221

them into the centre, so you have a single plait running down the centre of the tail and attached to it.

When the plait is about 8–12 ins/20–30 mm long (depending on the size of the horse or pony), do not take any more side hairs and continue the existing plait to the bottom of the hairs. This part should then be folded under and brought up to the point where the plait is 'joined' to the tail, and sewn in place. For added security you can thread the needle in and out down the first part of the plait as well.

THE LIBRARY
BISHOP BURTON COLLEGE
BEVERLEY HU17 8QG
TEL: 0964 550481 Ex: 227

CHAPTER 10

Notes on Stable Routine

Tying up

Whenever a horse is tied up whether in a stable or elsewhere, it must be tied wth some form of quick release knot, and if it is to be left unattended the rope should be tied to a piece of string, such as baler twine, attached to a fixed tie-ring. This is because if the horse should panic, or slip and fall, it could very easily break its neck unless quickly released; a piece of string, while being strong enough to convince the horse that it is securely tied, will break before any serious damage is done. This is particularly important if a nylon headcollar is used, as these have a much greater breaking strain than leather.

The tie-rope must be attached to the underside of the noseband of a headcollar, and under no circumstances should you tie a horse up to a bridle – the type of leather used for bridles is nowhere near

Quick release knot

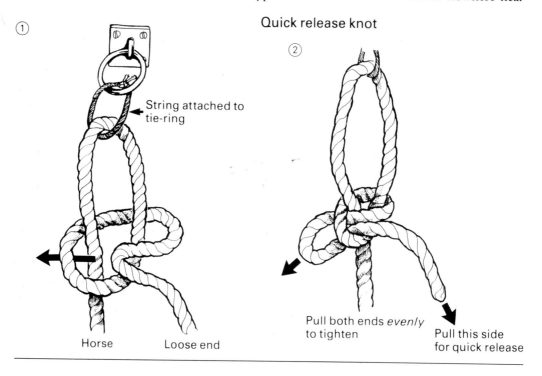

① String attached to tie-ring

Horse   Loose end

② Pull both ends *evenly* to tighten

Pull this side for quick release

strong enough for this purpose, and serious damage can be done to a horse's mouth if tied up by a rope attached to the bit.

The tie-ring must be at least on a level with the horse's nose; any lower and it would be possible for the horse to get a foot over the rope. If you always tie the horse up on a short rope there is again no danger of a 'loop' being formed over which the horse could get a foot.

Bedding

Wheat straw is a good bedding material as it is hard as well as hollow, so urine etc. will drain through it leaving the top layer dry.

Barley straw is often more commonly available, and is not now regarded with such disfavour it used to be; modern harvesting methods remove almost all of the prickly awns which can irritate a horse's skin. It is softer and flatter than wheat straw, however, and does not drain so well. It therefore does not last as long, but is usually cheaper to buy.

Oat straw is sometimes available in certain parts of the country, but it also does not drain well, and horses are inclined to eat it.

Wood shavings are another common bedding material, and the price varies from area to area – it is still sometimes possible to collect free shavings from large timber merchants or sawmills, but this is rapidly becoming a dying practice since the commercial potential has now been realised. The plastic bales in which they are packed make for easy transportation and storage, and availability is not governed by weather or seasons, as is that of straw.

One major advantage of straw over shavings or sawdust is that the manure is always easy to dispose of – most gardeners will be glad of it, and in some areas you may even be able to sell it.

Wet or soiled shavings soon begin to smell, so the stable must be thoroughly mucked out every day and droppings removed at frequent intervals. A special shavings fork will be necessary to enable you to sort out the wet shavings from the dry satisfactorily.

When you put the bed down for the night, make sure that all the straw is well shaken up, and that you bank the sides of the bed up the walls. This will make the bed much more comfortable for the horse – encouraging it to lie down and so rest its legs – and the air trapped between the layers of straw will make it warmer. Banking the sides applies to any bedding material since it will also help to prevent the horse getting cast as this practice encourages the horse to lie with its back close against the wall rather than facing it.

A horse is said to be cast (trapped) if it lies down too close to the wall and cannot stretch its legs out in order to get up, and although most horses do not lie down closely facing a wall, they do sometimes roll over and find themselves stuck. They then panic and are usually unable to roll back again to free themselves, often resulting in serious injury as they continue to struggle.

The bed should be thick enough so that the prongs of a fork will not strike through to the floor otherwise the horse can easily scrape and bruise its elbows and hocks when getting up and lying down. It is in any case false economy only to put in as little bedding as possible. You will actually discard no more dirty straw from a deep bed than from a shallow one as only the very bottom of the bed will be wet in either case.

With straw beds you have the choice of whether to muck out completely every day, or adopt a 'deep litter' system. In the latter case a deep bed of straw is laid, and thereafter only the droppings and very wet patches are removed on a daily basis, with fresh straw being placed on top. The whole bed is then mucked out thoroughly every couple of months or so.

The only disadvantage of this system is that very careful attention must be paid to the horse's feet as the deep bed will have a 'drawing' effect on them, making them soft and liable to bruising. A condition called 'thrush' (rotting of the frog) can also result. Adequate drainage must also be provided or the bed will quickly become soggy and foul-smelling.

Deep litter is, however, much warmer for the horse than a normal bed, and represents a considerable saving on time. It is worth considering if a horse is only to be stabled overnight and turned out by day – especially if time is at a premium – as in this way the horse would have the best of both worlds.

If your horse persistently eats its straw bed (and you are sure it is getting enough hay), either change to another form of bedding such as shavings, sawdust, peat moss or paper, or, if this is not possible, sprinkle a weak solution of Jeyes Fluid over the straw.

Horses with respiratory problems will usually have to be bedded on one of these alternative materials, since straw cannot be guaranteed to be free of dust.

Mucking out

The basic principles of mucking out apply to all bedding materials.

You will need a curved fork, a shovel and stiff yard brush; a pitchfork is also useful for shaking up and putting down straw. A builder's barrow is ideal for mucking out, particularly if the muck heap is any distance from the stable, as it is much easier to push when full and heavy than a garden barrow. A plastic laundry basket makes an ideal skip for removing droppings during the day – it is light and easy to carry, and also cannot harm the horse in the stable.

Mucking out is best done in the morning so that the stable floor has a chance to air and dry before the bed is put down for the night. If the horse is to remain in the stable, it must be tied up to prevent accidents with tools – or possible escape.

Remove all droppings and wet bedding, pile up the dry bedding against one wall, and sweep the floor before leaving it to air. If you pile the dry bedding against a different wall in turn each day, the whole box will be aired regularly.

Bedding material will go much further if you muck out carefully rather than indiscriminately throwing out large quantities with the droppings. With straw, slide the fork under the pile of droppings, take it to the barrow or skip and tilt the fork so that the droppings fall off leaving the clean straw behind – this is much easier and quicker than trying to shake droppings and soiled straw through the prongs of the fork as is sometimes recommended. After all the droppings have been removed, you will be left with one or more wet patches of straw on the floor; you need only remove the very wet straw from the bottom of these, the top is often dry enough to be re-used.

If a stable is mucked right out every day and the horse is kept in, you can leave the bulk of the bed up against a wall as normal, but always sprinkle a little straw (or shavings) over the floor. Horses do not like to stale (pass urine) on a bare floor, and they will either soil large amounts of bedding by dragging it down from the wall to stale on it or, more seriously, they can try to retain their urine.

When fresh straw is added, it should be put round the sides of the box since the middle is the area most frequently soiled. The next day, the straw from the sides can replenish that taken from the middle and so on; this will ensure that a good rotation is maintained with the minimum of waste.

The muck heap should be kept neat and tidy, and be box-shaped rather than a spreading mound. Not only does this look better but it will help the rotting process and keep flies to a minimum. If you get into the habit of squaring it off every day after mucking out, no extra work will be necessary to keep it under control. If space is at a premium, the heap can be 'stepped'. This is done by first forming a base layer, normally about 2 ft (60 cm) high with all edges squared off; the next layer (of the same thickness) covers perhaps two-thirds to three-quarters, leaving a step at the front, and so on. The front edges of the steps should be kept square – this is easily done by always putting the first few forkfuls along the front, rather than the back, of the step, and then levelling off when you finish. By forming steps in this way you will be able to make the heap much higher with a minimum of effort, as you can stand on a lower step to put manure on the highest one.

Rugging up

Any rug which is to be left on an unattended horse must be kept in place with a roller or, as with New Zealands and some of the modern rugs, its own surcingle. If a roller is used it must be well padded so that there is no pressure on the horse's spine, and should be tight enough to remain in place if the horse rolls or lies down, but not as tight as a girth.

When a rug is put on, it should be well forward leaving plenty of room at the front round the chest. It will tend to work its way back as the horse moves around, and if this is not taken into account to begin with, the rug may restrict the horse's movement and start to rub.

If you need to use one or more blankets under a stable rug to provide additional warmth, they should be as light as possible. Old-fashioned cellular blankets are ideal, as are lightweight pure wool ones. The underblankets should be laid over the horse so that they are in the right position on the body, but extend far up the neck, before being folded, as shown in the diagram. The roller holds everything in place, and the underblanket also ensures that the rug does not rub on the withers. There are several types of continental

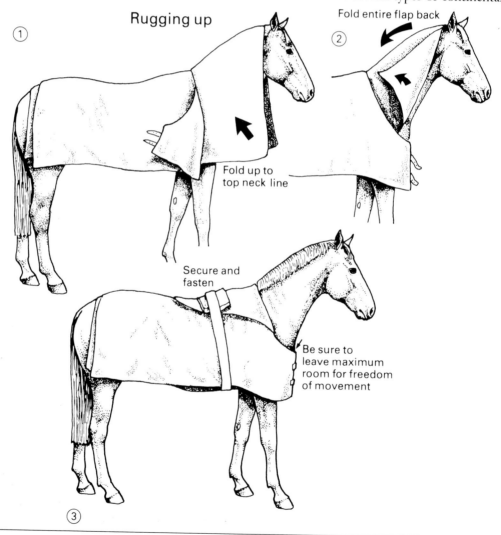

Rugging up

1

2 Fold entire flap back

Fold up to top neck line

Secure and fasten

Be sure to leave maximum room for freedom of movement

3

quilt type rugs available which supply sufficient warmth on their own, but by using blankets it is much easier to allow for changes in the weather as one (or more) layers can be removed or added as required. This is of particular help when 'roughing off' after the hunting season when the horse is to be turned out.

Watering

A stabled horse must have clean fresh water available at all times, except before fast work when it should be removed 1–2 hours beforehand.

Automatic drinkers can be fitted in stables, but they are expensive and do not allow you to monitor the amount of water being drunk over a given period, which can be important with fit competition horses. It is also difficult to add anything to the water (such as Epsom salts or medication prescribed by the vet) and, in winter, frozen – and subsequently burst – pipes are a constant hazard.

In the long run, the water bucket system takes some beating for overall efficiency, especially if the tap is nearby for ease of filling.

The horse's water should be changed completely twice or three times a day, as stale water quickly becomes unpalatable. Empty buckets, of course, must be refilled as necessary. Water plays a vital part in keeping the horse's digestive system functioning correctly, so you cannot afford to take chances – especially with a stabled horse whose diet largely consists of dry food.

Hay

Ideally, hay should be fed off the floor since this is the natural eating position of a horse when grazing. This also helps to prevent further development of the tough 'pulling' muscle under the neck, since the horse would have no reason to keep raising its head.

In practice, however, feeding hay in this way is extremely wasteful as most horses will scatter and trample it, thus rendering it unfit to eat.

A haynet or rack is the usual solution, but, if either is used, it must be high enough to prevent the horse from getting a foot caught if it paws the ground, but not so high that hay seeds will fall into the eyes.

Haynets should be tied to a piece of string attached to a stout ring about on a level with the top of the horse's head. The drawstring of the net is passed through a section from the base of the net before being pulled up tightly and tied with a quick-release knot. (See diagram on page 78.) This will prevent the bottom of the net from hanging down too low when empty.

Mangers

An old stone sink placed on the floor makes an ideal manger, since it is wide and shallow and has no sharp edges. All mangers must be kept scrupulously clean with all traces of previous feed removed before fresh feed is added. Not only would this otherwise encourage

Tying up of haynet

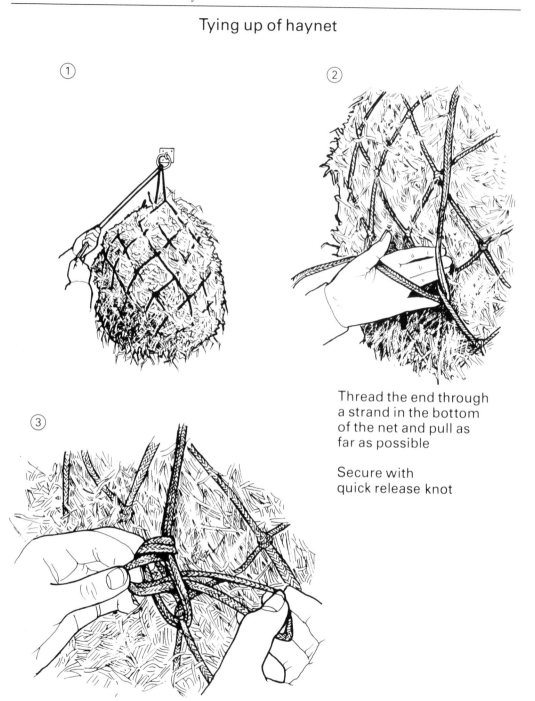

Thread the end through
a strand in the bottom
of the net and pull as
far as possible

Secure with
quick release knot

Pull both ends evenly to tighten and turn so
that the knot is at the back

vermin, but even the hungriest of horses will be put off by a sour-smelling manger.

Tack cleaning

Ideally, the tack should be rubbed over with a damp sponge every day after riding, and taken to pieces and thoroughly cleaned twice a week. In practice though, this rarely happens, and a good clean once a week is usually quite sufficient, unless it gets very muddy or caked with sweat. The bit, however, should be washed every day.

For the weekly clean, the bridle should be taken apart and girths and stirrups removed from the saddle.

A bucket of warm water (to which a dash of washing-up liquid has been added), a bar of saddle soap and two sponges will be required. The bit and stirrup irons should be put in the water to begin with and left to soak while the leather is cleaned; nylon string girths can also have the same treatment.

Without getting the leather soaking wet, it must be thoroughly sponged to remove all the scurf, grease and dirt.

The second sponge, which is used for soaping, must be practically dry so should not be put in the water. The end of the bar of soap should be dampened instead, as otherwise the sponge will start to froth, showing that it is too wet. Many people simply spit on the soap to moisten it, and reckon that this produces much better results.

Work the soap well into the sponge, and then rub it well into the leather – it should become soft, supple and shiny. Pay particular attention to places where the leather is folded – i.e. where the reins and cheekpieces are attached to the bit, the stirrup leathers where the iron passes through, and also where any buckles are habitually fastened. This is an ideal opportunity for you to check the condition of the tack, and repairs can be put in hand before something actually breaks.

Stainless steel bits and irons should only need washing with a sponge; a Brillo pad (used gently) will take care of any corrosion spots. Nickel irons can be cleaned with metal polish, but this must not be used on the mouthpiece of a bit unless it is well washed afterwards.

Nylon girths should be well scrubbed in soapy water, and then thoroughly rinsed before being dried. If any soap remains, it will make the girth hard, which will cause soreness and galling on the horse. For this reason nylon girths should not be dried by direct heat – over a radiator, for example – but must be allowed to dry naturally. This can be speeded up by first rolling the girth up in a towel which is then wrung out.

If the tack is to be stored for any length of time, the leather should be smeared with Vaseline to help keep it supple; oil should not be used as this will rot the stitching, and, to a certain extent, the leather.

CHAPTER 11

The Farrier

The term 'farrier' is used to describe a person trained and qualified to shoe horses; a 'blacksmith' has trained in iron work only. Along with the vet, the farrier is one of your most valuable allies. The old saying, 'No foot, no horse', is absolutely true – neglect of the horse's feet, or bad shoeing, will render the horse unridable as well as causing it considerable suffering.

If you are new to an area, it is worth asking others for the name of a good farrier. Nowadays, all farriers have to be registered with the Farriers Registration Council in order to practice, so if your local enquiries meet with unsatisfactory results, contact the Council (their address is on page 145), and it is also to them that any complaints concerning farriers should be made.

Good farriers are generally extremely busy, so if possible book an appointment at least two or three weeks before your horse's feet need attention. You may find that a farrier can fit you in more quickly if you travel to his forge.

When you make the appointment, tell the farrier what you think will need doing so he knows what to bring and how much time to allow for the visit. A trim will take about 15 minutes, while a 'refit' could be one to one and a half hours.

The horse's feet will require attention every six to eight weeks, whether shod or not, and, once a routine has been established, it is worth making a regular booking with the farrier, say, every six or seven weeks.

The obvious signs that a horse needs re-shoeing are:

(1) The clenches have risen so they are sticking out from the wall of the foot.

(2) The foot has grown too long so the shoes no longer fit correctly – the outside of the wall has started to grow down over the edge of the shoe.

(3) The shoe has worn thin in places (or all over). Once the groove running round the shoe (called fullering) has disappeared, the grip it provides is lost, and this can prove dangerous when riding on smooth roads. The nail heads will rapidly wear down too, and the

Structure of the foot

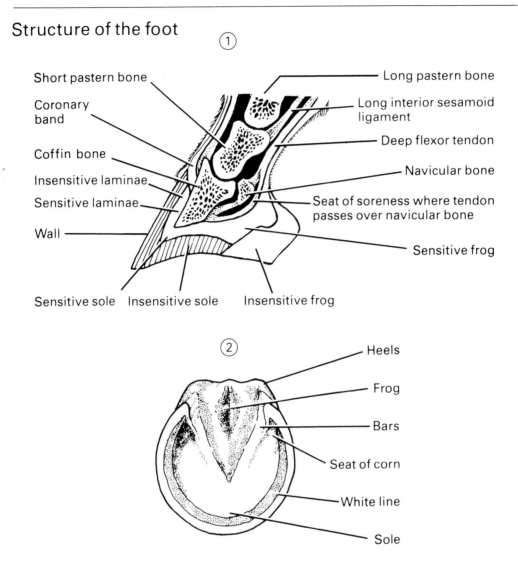

① Short pastern bone — Long pastern bone — Coronary band — Long interior sesamoid ligament — Coffin bone — Deep flexor tendon — Insensitive laminae — Navicular bone — Sensitive laminae — Seat of soreness where tendon passes over navicular bone — Wall — Sensitive frog — Sensitive sole — Insensitive sole — Insensitive frog

② Heels — Frog — Bars — Seat of corn — White line — Sole

shoe is much more likely to be pulled off leaving the nails embedded in the foot.

(4) The shoe is loose or twisted.

(5) If one shoe is lost.

(6) The horse is lame for no apparent reason – your vet would advise you on this.

If shoes are left on longer than seven or eight weeks without being removed and the feet trimmed, the feet will get 'pinched' and corns will result.

The feet of a grass-kept horse will usually grow more rapidly than those of a stabled horse, especially during the spring and summer, so these horses will need the farrier's attention more frequently – probably every five or six weeks, whether shod or not, as the feet will still require trimming.

When you first contact a farrier who has not previously seen the horse, he may ask you to measure the feet. This is best done with a steel (or plastic) measure rather than a tape, and the measurements required are from the outside heel to the toe, and the width of the foot across its widest point, measured on the sole. (See diagram.)

Measuring the foot

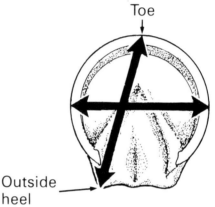

Toe

Outside
heel

From these measurememts he will be able to make up shoes which should be a good fit, but if at all possible have the horse shod 'hot' the first time at least, until the farrier gets to know the size and shape of the feet.

The benefits of 'hot' shoeing over 'cold' are great: not only can the farrier ensure a perfect fit by altering the shape and length of the shoe, but also by 'burning' it on, he can see that the foot is perfectly level and the shoe straight before it is nailed on. If for any reason he wishes to change the position of the nail holes, this can also be easily done; also stud holes are put in while the shoe is red hot.

Many farriers have portable electric or gas forges which enable them to make major adjustments to the shoes. With 'cold' shoeing, however, only very small alterations can be made – and one of the most important rules of shoeing is that the shoe must be made to fit the foot, not vice versa.

Although some young horses take a while to become accustomed to the noise and atmosphere of the forge, and the smoke rising from their hooves when a red hot shoe is burned on, it is surprising how quickly they accept this procedure once that realise it doesn't hurt.

You will save money by taking the horse to the forge, as the farrier's travelling fee is based not only on the distance to your home but on the length of time he takes to reach you. However, it is sometimes possible to economise on travelling by organising a visit to more than one horse in the same area on the same day. In this respect, and in order to make sure the farrier will be able to come out when you need him, forward planning is essential.

Obviously an emergency is different – you will have to persuade the farrier to look at the horse as soon as possible. If, for example, a horse has twisted a shoe it cannot be left too long. Most farriers are more amenable to urgent requests if they know you normally plan well in advance.

If your farrier has agreed to come out to do a particular job, don't spring surprises on him. 'While you are here, could you just . . . .?' is not a good question to ask, as he will not have allowed for extra tasks in his schedule. If he stays longer to do an additional job it is not fair on the next customer, for whom he will be late. If, after having made the appointment, you discover that another horse will need attention, or you want special shoes or studs, you should ring him up before he comes out; in this way he can plan accordingly.

You should have the horse brought in, and its feet cleaned and picked out, in plenty of time for the farrier's visit, as he will not appreciate being kept waiting.

If possible, the horse should be shod in a stable from which the bedding has been removed; (a) because of the fire risk if the horse is to be 'hot' shod, and (b) because the farrier will need to see the horse standing on a clean, hard, level surface when he has trimmed the feet. It should, in theory, be easier to keep the horse under control in a stable than in a field, and both farrier and horse will be protected from the elements. You will normally be expected to remain with the horse to keep it under proper control.

The horse must be kept still while the farrier is working; apart from making life easier all round, the consequences can be serious if the horse, for example, puts a foot down while the shoe is being taken off or nailed on. Since you cannot reasonably expect a horse to know when it is safe to move or not, you should teach it to stand still all the time.

If it is inclined to fidget, a haynet might help to keep it occupied, but it is not a good idea to feed titbits since this will encourage it to keep looking for more, and it may well try to bite you or the farrier when thwarted.

If you are unable to tie it up, and you feel that you do not have sufficient control with a headcollar, put on a bridle and attach a rope to the bit ring on the far side. Bring the rope over the poll and pass it through the nearside bit ring (towards you).

When the farrier has one front foot up on the tripod in front of the horse, his back will be just under the horse's nose – don't allow it to

THE LIBRARY
BISHOP BURTON COLLEGE
BEVERLEY HU17 8QG
TEL 0964 550481 Ex 227

nibble, even though you may be confident that it will not actually bite; most farriers are extremely annoyed by horses which do this, and by owners who permit it.

Finally, it is worth bearing in mind that the farrier will know much more about horses' feet than you do. He will not appreciate being told how to do his job, and may tend to get touchy if he thinks you are criticising, so any queries must be put tactfully. Farriers are also not keen about taking on another's work, particularly if remedial work has been started, so once you have found a good farrier, don't lose him!

There are a few things you can look out for which will give you an indication that he has done a good job:

(1) There must be no 'daylight' between the foot and the shoe.

(2) The shoe must have been made to fit the foot, and not the foot to fit the shoe (particularly if the horse has been 'cold' shod).

(3) The clenches (the ends of the nails visible on the wall of the foot) should be in a straight line and flush with the wall.

(4) The angle of the foot should be comparable with that of the pastern – i.e. the toe should not be so long or the heels so high that the slope of the foot is altered.

(5) The wall should not have been excessively rasped – the only rasping necessary is a small amount over the clenches to ensure a flush fit, and only to the very edge of the toe.

(6) The toe has not been 'dumped' – i.e. cut off to make a shoe fit which is basically too short.

(7) The heels of the shoe must not be too long, i.e. extending past the heel of the foot. In the case of front shoes, this would increase the risk of the horse pulling the shoe off with the hind foot, or cause it to stumble.

(8) The frog should be in contact with the ground, as it acts as a shock-absorber for the foot and assists the circulation of blood within it.

(9) The weight of shoe reflects the size of the horse and the work done with it. Horse shoes can be made from varying weights of metal, the lighter weights being used for ponies and small horses which do not undergo much road work, and so on up the scale. Too heavy a shoe can adversely affect the horse's action, and too light a shoe will wear out quickly. A set of shoes should last for twelve to fourteen weeks on a horse doing only a moderate amount of road work with not much trotting, but the shoes will have to be removed and refitted at least once during that period.

(10) Last, but by no means least, the horse must not be lame after shoeing. If it is, the offending shoe must be removed immediately, as if the sensitive laminae have been pierced ('pricked') by a nail, for instance, infection will build up very quickly and the horse could be lame for months. It is extremely unlikely that a reputable farrier

would 'prick' a horse, unless perhaps the horse had misbehaved at a critical moment while the shoe was being nailed on. A nail passing very close to the sensitive laminae (called nail 'bind') may not make the horse noticeably lame until the next day, but this is one occasion when you would be justified in demanding prompt attendance by the farrier.

CHAPTER 12

Routine Veterinary Care

Worming

All horses have a certain number of worms in their system, but they must be rigorously controlled in order to avoid damage to the stomach and intestines. Large numbers of worms can also cause colic, and even death.

There are two main types of worms which commonly infest horses: ascarids (roundworm) and strongyles (redworm, lungworm, threadworm and whipworm).

Of these, roundworms, which may be seen in the droppings of a badly infested horse and can be up to 4–6 ins (10–15 cm) in length, do the least damage as they take nourishment from the horse's food, but do not attach themselves to the stomach or intestines. Their effect will be mainly to cause the horse to lose condition, and large numbers of big worms are often found in young horses. (A heavy concentration of roundworms can, however, cause a blockage or colic.)

Severe infestation should be suspected if a horse has a dull coat, its ribs are clearly visible, it has a pot belly and is inexplicably lethargic – especially if it is known to have been turned out to grass in a relatively small field, either on its own or with other horses, for several months or more with little in the way of regular attention from its owner.

The strongyle family are much more dangerous. All these worms are very small and are rarely seen in the droppings, although threadworms, pinworms and whipworms can sometimes be seen round the anus in the form of a sticky discharge, where they cause intense irritation and severe itching.

Redworms, which are in fact grey in colour, are probably the most dangerous, as they will work their way through the intestines, through the liver to the lungs and into the blood system where they can cause thrombosis; they also damage the walls of the intestines and cause abscesses and growths.

Lungworms are not commonly found among horses unless kept with donkeys, which are particularly prone to them. They are extremely dangerous as they work through into the lungs where they damage the air sacs and also cause congestion; a severe infestation will ruin a horse's wind very quickly if unchecked. These worms are passed out in the urine.

Broadly, the method of infestation is much the same for most of the more common types of worms. The worm eggs are passed in the dung and then hatch into larvae in the open (somes larvae are also passed). These larvae have a hard protective sheath and can withstand sun, frost and drying – they can lie dormant for up to a year. They are eaten by the horse along with the grass, and shed the protective sheath in the warmth of the saliva. They then work their way through the system to their preferred place of residence, taking nourishment all the way, and reach adult form, when they lay eggs and the cycle is repeated.

Cross-grazing with sheep or cattle will break this cycle, as the eggs and larvae of equine worms are destroyed in the intestines of these animals, but, even so, regular worming of the horse must still be carried out.

Bots are another parasite which infests horses, and which can be controlled by the use of certain of the 'worm' preparations available. They are the product of the gadfly, which lays its eggs on the horse's legs (or on the grass when the eggs are brushed off on to the legs of the horse as it moves through long grass) and can be seen as tiny yellow or white specks stuck to the hairs. These are licked off by the horse, and hatch in the mouth; they travel to the stomach where they attach themselves to the lining and cause abscesses and inflammation. The stomach swells around the bot, and the horse may show several symptoms of severe digestive disorder.

The eggs should be removed with paraffin or a razor blade, and a worm preparation containing an agent against bots used twice or three times a year in rotation with the ordinary doses.

Worm preparations come in powder or granular form to be mixed with the horse's feed, or as a paste contained in a plastic syringe which enables you to squirt it down the horse's throat.

If a 'new' horse seems to be severely infested and is in very poor condition, it is better to ask the vet for advice, as he may prefer to administer a stronger preparation via a stomach tube.

Powder or granules are cheaper than paste, and provided the horse will eat the 'doctored' feed (a strong-tasting mineral supplement can be used to disguise the smell and flavour of the powder) they are quite adequate.

To dose with paste, stand at the side of the horse, and with one hand holding the front of the nose (so that the horse cannot move forward), take the syringe in the other and insert it into the corner of the mouth. The nozzle should point down the throat as far back as possible. (These syringes are graduated to control the amount given to horses of different bodyweights, so the setting should be checked before you start.) Press the plunger firmly so that the paste is expelled smoothly and all in one go, keeping the horse's head up for several seconds afterwards. If you haven't placed the nozzle far enough back in the mouth, you will find that the horse will spit the paste straight out again – probably all over you.

It is often a good idea to stand the horse with its back to a wall or fence as it may well try and makes its escape in reverse.

An inviting titbit offered immediately afterwards will encourage the horse to swallow properly, and ensures that all the paste goes down.

Horses living out should be wormed every six to eight weeks, more frequently (four to six weeks) if the paddock is small and not cross-grazed. Stabled horses need only be wormed every eight to ten weeks as they are not so likely to be re-infested so quickly, and if the horse is kept in during the night and out in the day (or vice versa) every seven to eight weeks.

Removal of the bulk of the droppings from the field will certainly help to keep the level of worm infestation down, but to be really effective this needs to be done every two or three days, which is often not practicable. Regular worming with varying preparations will normally do just as well, but since eggs and larvae can survive for long periods, as many droppings as possible should be removed before the field is harrowed, and only very well-rotted manure should be used as fertiliser.

After worming, the horse should be kept in the stable for twenty-four hours before being turned out again, to avoid immediate re-contamination of the pasture. If no stable is available, a small corner of the field can be fenced off to confine the horse, and all the droppings passed during this period removed and burned.

Although modern worm preparations are not nearly so 'fierce' as they used to be years ago, it is still not a good idea to worm the horse the day before a competition or other fast work; worming can usually be arranged for the day before a rest day with no disruption to the work schedule, and the horse will probably then have a week to get back to peak form.

One final point: the correct quantity of all worm preparations is governed by the horse's weight, and the effectiveness is dangerously reduced if you consistently under-dose. The easiest, and most accurate, way to determine the weight is to take the horse in a trailer to a public weighbridge – or even ride it there.

The trailer can be weighed with the horse on board, and then with the horse taken out; alternatively, if the horse will stand still, you can have it weighed, standing directly on the weighbridge – but don't forget to deduct your own weight!

If this is impossible, use the following formula to gauge the horse's weight, but remember that it won't be exact.

$$\frac{G^2 \times L}{300} = \text{weight in lbs (G = girth; L = length)}$$

The length (measured in inches, as in the girth) is taken from the point of shoulder to the tuber ischii (point of buttocks); if desired, the answer can then be converted to kilograms. Note: the formula does *not* work if you take the measurements in centimetres; you must convert the final figure only to kilograms.

Vaccinations

The most important routine vaccination is against tetanus, which should on no account be neglected as this dreadful disease is almost always fatal.

Any form of puncture wound (where the wound is small in area but deep, as with thorns etc. in the feet or legs) can harbour the tetanus germ. The bacillus is killed by contact with the air, but thrives in wounds where the original 'hole' in the skin has closed over; from there it finds its way into the blooodstream. The disease is more prevalent in certain geographical areas; local farmers and the vet will be able to tell you about your particular locality.

Two primary vaccinations are given about a month apart, and thereafter, an annual booster is advisable to ensure adequate protection, but in the event of a puncture wound of any kind, check that the vaccinations are up to date. If not, or you are not sure, the vet will give an injection of anti-tetanus serum which will give temporary protection to cover the period while the wound is healing.

Any horse due to have its booster should be thoroughly checked over beforehand to make sure that it has no hitherto undetected puncture wounds when the vaccination is given. The injection contains a small amount of live vaccine which encourages the horse's system to build up antibodies to fight it; if a puncture wound exists and tetanus bacilli are present within it, there is a chance that the horse might contract the disease immediately after the vaccination – a remote chance, but, again, it is pointless to take the risk.

If the horse is to compete or hunt regularly, it is also worth immunising it against equine influenza. Some competitions require proof that this has been done as a condition of entry. It is a sensible precaution to take if your horse regularly comes into contact with others since it is a highly infectious disease and permanent damage to the horse's wind can result.

The vaccination against influenza is normally carried out at the same time as that against tetanus, using a combined vaccine, and the same principles apply: two primary injections followed by an annual booster, and any horse which is coughing already should not be vaccinated until completely well again.

Care of the teeth

When you contact the vet to make the appointment for the vaccinations, ask him to bring with him equipment for rasping the horse's teeth. A dental check-up is the other annual requirement which should not be forgotten, since many problems can arise through sharp teeth or sore gums.

Horses' teeth are continually wearing down, and it is quite common for the wear to be uneven, leading to sharp edges which can set up inflammation in the gums.

The horse's jaws are prised apart by means of a Hauptman gag (which fits over the head and into the mouth) so that the vet can reach inside and make a thorough examination of all the teeth and rasp off any sharp edges.

Apart from the obvious effect of sharp teeth, i.e. the food not being properly chewed, there are several other problems which may well be solved by a look in the horse's mouth.

A horse which is normally well-behaved when ridden may start to toss its head, raise and carry it high, tilt it to one side or lean on the bit – in fact any unusual behaviour with the head can indicate that there is something wrong in the mouth, and an inspection by the vet should be the first course of action.

Similarly if the horse suddenly starts to object when you try to put a bridle on it, or is discovered to be spitting out mouthfuls of food (called 'quidding'), or even begins to leave part of its feed regularly, sharp and/or troublesome teeth are often the cause.

As well as the permanent teeth, some horses have 'wolf teeth', just in front of the back teeth (molars), which are a relic of an earlier stage in their evolution. These wolf teeth are not present in all horses, as they are often shed with the milk teeth when young, but if they remain they can catch on the bit and generally annoy the horse while being ridden. They should be removed by the vet – usually a fairly easy job as wolf teeth have very little root.

CHAPTER 13

Routine Care of Horses at Grass

All horses living out must be checked once, but preferably twice, a day. If you think about it, should a horse suffer an injury half an hour after you leave, 23½ hours is a very long time to wait for treatment.

Spring/summer

In summer, the daily inspection should include: looking for injury or illness, picking out the feet, making sure that the horse is not too bothered by flies and has shelter available, watching to see that it does not get too fat, maintaining a clean water supply and making sure the fencing is intact.

Once a week you should walk round the field to check the fencing thoroughly and make sure that there are no 'foreign' objects in the field – particularly if it is near to habitation or adjacent to a road or footpath.

If you are working, or otherwise occupied during the day, you may well want to ride in the summer evenings, but you must remember that the horse must not be returned to the field while hot and sweating as it can easily get chilled. You should plan to walk the last mile or so if you have been doing any fast work, so that the horse is cool before you turn it out. Temperatures can drop quite alarmingly after dusk, even in the summer.

If a hard feed is to be given (and it should not be necessary unless the horse is in fast work or starts to lose weight), feed in the evening: (a) as a reward after work, and (b) to help the horse to keep warm overnight.

If the horse is being pestered by flies during the day, and it is not possible to stable it for a few hours to gain some respite, you can either apply a fly-repellant, taking care to avoid the eyes and nostrils, or fit a fly-fringe – a browband on which strings about 6 ins (15 cm) long are knotted – to the headcollar. This will at least keep the flies away from the horse's eyes. Proprietary fly-tags, used by farmers for cattle, can be clipped on to the headcollar or plaited into the mane near the poll. Allow the horse's tail to grow longer than normal, and this, too, will help keep flies at bay.

You may well have been told that a horse's feet should be cold, and this is quite true – but if a horse has either been galloping round the

Fly fringe

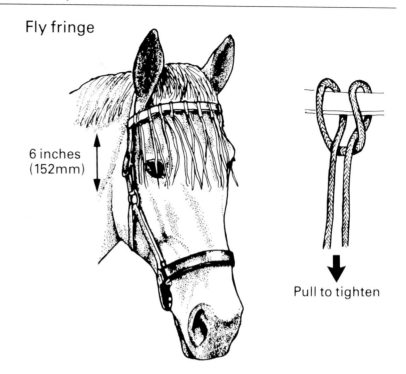

6 inches
(152mm)

Pull to tighten

field or standing still in one spot for any length of time, its feet might
be slightly warm. After an hour or so, they should have cooled down
(unless the weather is very hot); if not, pick up each foot in turn and
tap the walls and sole sharply with a hoofpick. Any flinching should
be regarded with suspicion, and the horse should be trotted up and
its action carefully watched.

Any signs of lameness, 'going short' (i.e. taking shorter strides
than normal with one or more legs), stumbling or unusual unwillingness to move would indicate that veterinary attention is required
– particularly if the horse has been grazing on rich grass since it
could well be the onset of laminitis (fever of the feet) – see Chapter
15 'Your Horse's Health'.

Careful daily observation will soon establish a pattern; some
horses will often have slightly warm feet, while others never do
unless they are injured.

One foot whch feels much warmer than all the others is a different
matter – especially when it is accompanied by lameness. Any such
must be investigated without delay as prompt veterinary attention is
essential in all cases of infection in the foot.

One last thing to look out for, especially if the horses graze with or
near cattle, is the appearance of small round lumps on the back (or
occasionally elsewhere on the body) from February/March until
about June/July. These are the product of the warble fly, which lays

its eggs on the skin of the horse's legs. The eggs hatch into maggots which bore into the skin and work through the system until they appear as lumps under the skin on the back. Here they grow rapidly, feeding on the pus exuded by the wound they have made, until they are mature when they bore another hole through the skin and emerge from it.

If warbles do appear on the horse's back they are best left alone as trying to speed up the process can result in killing the maggot which then sets up a considerable infection. If they are present on the saddle patch, on no account should the horse be ridden for the same reason. Under normal circumstances the 'ripening' process will take four to five days from the time when the lump first appears; if it is vital that the horse is worked, you can apply warm cloths or pads to the affected area to speed things up a little, but care must be taken that the fomentations are not too hot. The horse can be lunged, but no part of the tack must come into contact with the lump.

The only preventative measure you can take is to treat the horse with cattle wash, obtainable from the vet or an agricultural merchant, from May to August when the warble fly lays its eggs.

Autumn/winter

In winter, you will have to check the horse twice a day, and each time remove the ice from the water supply in freezing weather. Additionally the New Zealand rug shuld be adjusted if it has slipped, and the horse checked over for any sign of the rug or straps rubbing.

Check that the horse is warm enough by holding the base of the ears; in very cold wet weather you should be able to feel the body heat coming through to your fingers within about ten seconds – if it still feels icy cold after that time, and the horse's back feels cold under the rug, it should either be brought in or, if this is not possible, another rug put on underneath the New Zealand.

Generally speaking, a horse which is shivering really is cold – it is unlikely to be 'putting it on', and it will also look thoroughly miserable. Its back will be hunched, giving a 'tucked up' appearance – its belly looks tense and drawn up – and the tail will be firmly clamped down.

Some horses will always look miserable when it is raining, whether they are really cold or not, but you will learn to recognise when additional warmth is required, and when it can safely be left to get on with it.

It is a fact that horses which live out all the time are much less likely to suffer from coughs, colds and chills – it is only when they are stabled, or partly stabled, that they become more prone to these conditions.

Remember that the grass will have very little feed value through the winter, so it is vital that the horse is given enough to eat. The food it consumes will do more to keep it warm than any number of rugs. Hay should be put out twice a day, morning and evening, and the daily hard feed ration split into two – the larger amount being given in the evening.

Hay can be fed from the ground, but this tends to be extremely wasteful. If there are any suitable trees in the field, permission can be sought from the farmer to hammer a large staple into one of them to which a haynet can be attached, but you must ask first as this practice is not always approved. Or you could ask if he has an old rack or feeder which you could use. These are normally made of wood or metal and are free standing; the hay is placed inside and the horse draws it out through the bars in the sides. Whatever its construction make sure it has no sharp edges.

There is no doubt that a hot feed is welcomed by horses living out in very cold weather. Bear in mind, though, that any mineral supplement loses much of its value unless added after the feed has cooled a little.

The water supply must be maintained at all costs in the winter, as the horse's diet consists largely of dry forage which requires large amounts of water to enable proper digestion to take place. You will find that the horse will drink considerably more water at this time of year than in the spring when eating mostly fresh grass.

In wet weather, particularly if the field tends to become boggy, watch the feet and legs carefully for signs of thrush, mud fever or cracked heels. These are not serious conditions in themselves, but can become so if neglected.

Thrush is characterised by a foul, rotten smell from the foot accompanied by a black discharge from the soft, spongy frog. It is commonly found in horses living on wet land or standing in deep, wet bedding. Clean the foot thoroughly with neat hydrogen per-oxide and ask the vet or blacksmith to cut away the rotten areas of frog. Pack the foot with cotton wool (liberally smeared with Stockholm tar), and change the dressing every day; the condition should clear up within a week or ten days.

Mud fever, apparent as festering scabs on the lower legs and pasterns, is a bacterial infection also common in cold, wet weather and a cure can only be effected by killing the bacteria with antibiotics and keeping the area dry. Vaseline smeared on to clean, dry legs *before* they become infected is a wise precaution, but if mud fever does occur, veterinary advice should always be sought.

Cracked heels, as the name suggests, affect the fleshy parts of the heels and is a similar condition to chapped hands in humans. Zinc and castor oil cream, or Vaseline, should be applied to the affected area after first drying it thoroughly.

You will have to exercise your discretion in late autumn and early spring to decide when to start – and stop – using a New Zealand rug. Obviously all will depend on the weather and access to a local forecast is invaluable. On the whole, it is better to err on the side of caution and leave the rug on if in doubt, particularly at the end of the winter when the horse's system has become accustomed to the protection it affords.

A horse rugged early in the autumn will not grow such a thick winter coat, which is a blessing if you want to ride through the winter but a drawback if it has to live out completely. At the end of the winter, the longer a rug is left on, the sooner the horse will have its summer coat – again, a blessing if you are riding, but a drawback when the rug is then removed as the horse's coat will afford no protection from cold wet weather in late spring. As a compromise, begin by using the rug at night, and during the day only if the weather is cold and wet; the same applies to roughing off at the end of the winter. A horse which is too hot under a rug will sweat slightly; take this as an indication that the rug is not necessary.

You may find that the horse will lose some condition after the rug has been left off completely, but provided that you are sure that the horse is not cold and is being adequately fed, there is no need for undue concern. Spring grass will quickly put matters to rights.

Take care, though, that condition is not lost for any reason in the autumn if the horse is to live out. It is notoriously difficult to put flesh on through the winter, so, in this case, slightly too fat is better than too thin.

CHAPTER 14

Boots and Bandages

Apart from the occasions when used under direction from the vet, boots and bandages have two functions: (1) to support, and (2) to protect.

Exercise bandages

Exercise bandages, made from elastic material, are still widely used to support the tendons of horses doing hard or fast work (such as jumping) when the ground is hard. They must always be used with Gamgee underneath to cushion them, as they will otherwise restrict the blood supply.

A suitably sized piece of Gamgee should be cut from the roll, to

Fitting an exercise bandage

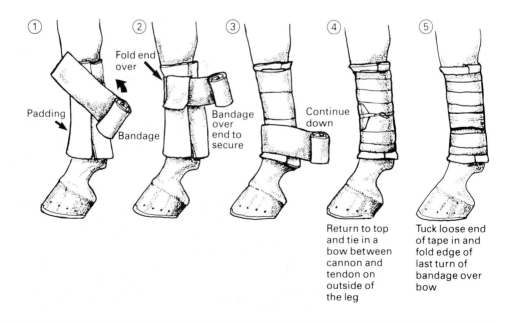

① Padding — Bandage

② Fold end over — Bandage over end to secure

③ Continue down

④ Return to top and tie in a bow between cannon and tendon on outside of the leg

⑤ Tuck loose end of tape in and fold edge of last turn of bandage over bow

cover the leg from just below the knee or hock to the fetlock, with an overlap of about 1 in (25 mm) down the side of the leg, and allowing the same amount above and below the bandage. (If the horse is to be worked in clean conditions, the Gamgee can be re-used several times. Stitch round the cut edge with a large blanket stitch to help it keep its shape and stop it from disintegrating.) There is now a new, light material (called Fybagee) which can be used instead of Gamgee and is not so bulky.

Before you start to bandage, make sure that you have everything to hand and that the bandage is correctly rolled – with the tapes to the centre of the roll. Hold the Gamgee round the leg, with the 'joined' edges to the outside and the overlap pointing towards the

EXERCISE BANDAGE – the knot is on the outside of the leg, between cannon and tendon, and the bandage is evenly wound with no wrinkles. The padding is showing above and below the bandage to avoid any rubbing, and the tapes have been neatly tucked out of the way.

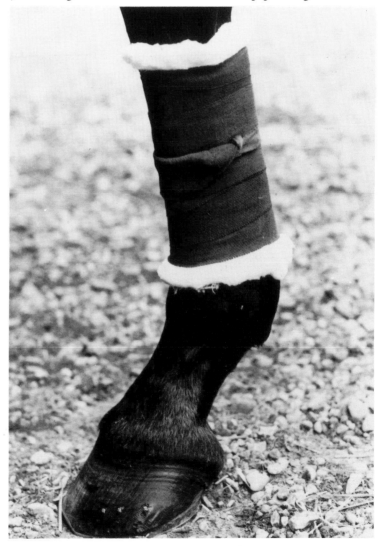

rear of the horse. Fybagee is wound round the leg in the same way as a bandage. Start bandaging about 1½–2 ins (37–50 mm) below the bottom of the knee or hock, taking the first couple of turns upwards to secure the loose edge as shown in the diagram, and keep the bandage parallel to the ground, free from wrinkles or tucks and with an even tension throughout. In order to be of any benefit as support for the tendons the bandage must be fairly tight and cover the whole area from knee (or hock) to fetlock. Leaving the top and bottom of the Gamgee exposed will ensure that there is no 'sharp edge' of bandage which could restrict circulation. You should always bandage the tendons inwards – in other words when working on the nearside of the horse you would be bandaging anticlockwise, and, on the offside, clockwise. This will make sure that the tendons are supported correctly, and not pulled out of line by the bandage as it is applied.

Ideally, the bandage should finish where you started, but should, in any case, be near the top for safety and with practice you will become accustomed to the length of the bandage and the way in which it goes on.

To finish, pass the tapes round the leg once more (no tighter than the actual bandage) and tie them with a bow on the outside of the leg between the cannon bone and tendon. On no account should this be otherwise – even if it means taking it off and starting again – since a knot of any kind will bruise the cannon bone or tendon, and could get caught by the opposite foot if done on the inside of the leg.

The loose ends of the bow should be tucked into the tape, and the top half of the last 'turn' of the bandage pulled down to cover it.

If exercise bandages are to be used when jumping across country, they should additionally be sewn in place, and sticky tape wound over the last couple of turns for extra security.

It is not a good idea to use exercise bandages as a matter of course during normal work, unless directed by the vet, as the tendons will come to 'rely' on them for support, and can become weakened. They should be used on the forelegs when jumping if the ground is hard as they will reduce the conscussion through the legs as the horse lands.

Although various types of tendon boots and 'competition' boots are now widely available, a properly applied exercise bandage is still the best means of support.

If ever one leg is bandaged for any reason, the corresponding leg must also be bandaged or the horse will be inclined to 'favour' one or the other.

Brushing boots

If a horse is inclined to brush, that is, strike the inside of one leg, usually around the fetlock area, with the fetlock or foot of the other, brushing boots should be used. These are now made from a variety of materials, including leather, and have a reinforced pad running

BRUSHING BOOTS
— these will protect the inside of the leg and fetlock joint from knocks and should fit snugly. The fastenings face towards the back.

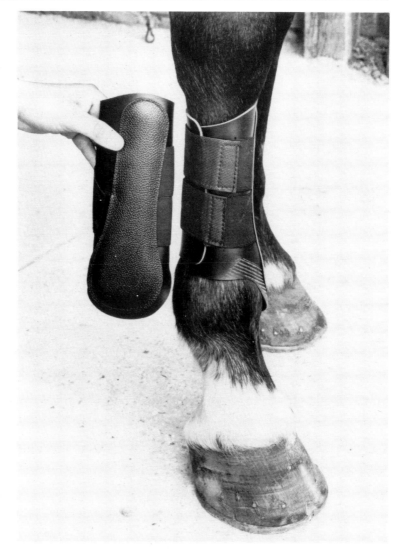

down the inside of each leg to guard against injury. They also come in varying sizes and shapes and are secured by straps and buckles or Velcro strips facing the rear, on the outside of the leg.

When brushing boots are used or indeed any boots, you must make sure that there are no bits of mud or other debris inside them which would cause an irritation to the horse, and that they fit properly. Since they are worn without the protection of Gamgee underneath, care must be taken to ensure that the edges do not dig in, that they are tight enough to ensure that they cannot slip round, but not so tight that the circulation is restricted.

TENDON AND OVERREACH BOOTS – tendon boots are often worn by showjumpers to protect the back of the leg – especially the tendon – in the event of a horse striking into itself as it lands over a fence. Worn in conjunction with overreach boots, as here, the heels are also protected.

Overreach boots

Overreach boots are made of rubber, and are either the pull-on variety or have some kind of strap or Velcro fastening. They fit over the hoof around the pastern and, as their name implies, are designed to protect the heels of the horse from an overreach injury, caused when the toe of a hind foot strikes into the heel of a forefoot. They should always be used if the horse is jumping, and particularly when the going is at all tricky as the horse may well slip and become unbalanced.

The pull-on type can be quite a struggle to put on and take off, but at least there is no danger of them coming undone in use. They fit loosely and comfortably round the pastern and have no fastening which could be caught by the opposite foot. To put them on, firstly turn them inside out with the widest part uppermost and pull them over the hoof. The top is then turned down to fit over the foot.

These boots can also be used when the horse is travelling, as they will protect the coronet from a 'tread' – this is one of the most common travelling injuries, and happens when the horse loses balance and treads on the opposite foot.

Travelling boots

Travelling boots, which extend from below the knee or hock, are very often not long enough; they do not always cover the coronet and so do not really fulfil their purpose – hence the suggestion that overreach boots should be worn as well. Travelling boots are, however, much quicker to put on and take off than stable bandages, which can be an important consideration if you are on your own at a show or hunting 'meet' with an excited horse.

It is quite possible to make your own travelling boots out of tough canvas (or similar material), simulated sheepskin for padding and Velcro for the fastenings. Not only will this save you money, but the boots can be made to fit your horse perfectly. The design shown will also protect the knee and hock.

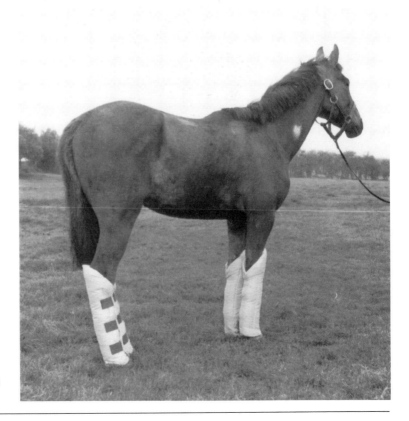

TRAVELLING BOOTS – this design protects the knees and hocks as well as the legs, and continues down over the coronet.

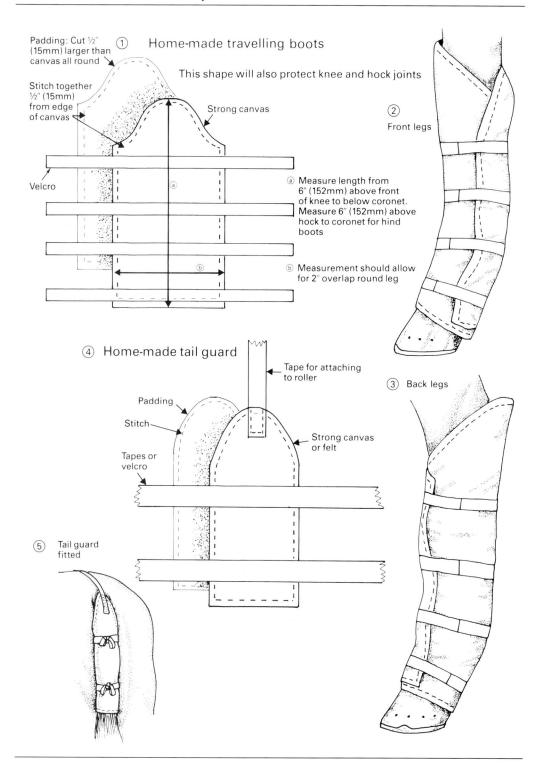

Padding: Cut ½" (15mm) larger than canvas all round

① Home-made travelling boots

This shape will also protect knee and hock joints

Stitch together ½" (15mm) from edge of canvas

Strong canvas

② Front legs

Velcro

ⓐ

ⓑ

ⓐ Measure length from 6" (152mm) above front of knee to below coronet. Measure 6" (152mm) above hock to coronet for hind boots

ⓑ Measurement should allow for 2" overlap round leg

④ Home-made tail guard

Padding

Stitch

Tapes or velcro

Tape for attaching to roller

Strong canvas or felt

③ Back legs

⑤ Tail guard fitted

Knee and hock boots

The knees and hocks should always be protected when travelling, and if the travelling boots do not extend to cover these areas, special boots will be necessary – particularly on a young or nervous horse which can easily lose balance or slip on the ramp. Knee boots should be fitted with the top strap fairly tight or the boots will slip down the leg. Obviously it must not be so tight that it interferes with the circulation – or comfort – of the horse, particularly if a long journey is to be undertaken. The bottom strap should be left very loose so that the horse can flex its knee.

Hock boots are fitted on the same principles, i.e. with the top strap tighter than the bottom, but the top should not be as tight as that on the knee boots.

Tail bandages

Tail bandages, made of the same material as exercise bandages, are used to protect the tail from rubbing while travelling as most horses like to lean against the back ramp; they should also be put on after the tail is washed to keep it clean and the hairs flat and in place.

Starting at the top, bandage down the tail to the end of the bone, keeping the bandage straight and the pressure even. The fault most commonly seen is that the tail bandage is put on too tight. Obviously it must be firm enough to stop it from being rubbed loose or slipping down, but if too tight it cuts off the blood circulation and also damages the hairs.

As with all bandages, it should finish near the top. Again, much will depend on your expertise and the length of the bandage. The tapes should be passed once round the tail before being tied in a bow, the loose ends tucked in and the top half of the last turn of bandage folded over. The tapes must never be any tighter than the bandage.

For added protection when travelling a tail guard can be improvised from a piece of felt or similar material cut to shape as shown, and some tape.

Stable bandages

Stable bandages, made from woollen material, cover the same area as travelling boots – from just below the knee or hock to below the coronet – and are used with Gamgee underneath in the same way as exercise bandages. Apart from giving protection when travelling, stable bandages also provide warmth and comfort to a tired horse.

Since they are not elastic, they must not be put on too tightly, and although they are bulkier the same technique and principles apply to these as to exercise bandages except that only one corner is folded down when you begin.

Since most stable bandages are rarely long enough, and the cheaper ones are made from synthetic material rather than wool, these are another item which can profitably be made by yourself from woollen material such as an old blanket.

Fitting a stable bandage

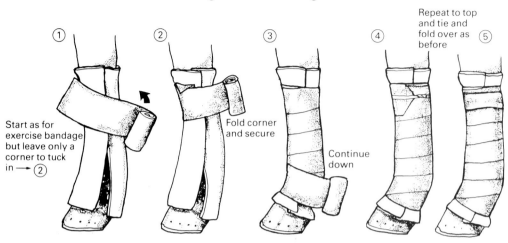

① Start as for exercise bandage but leave only a corner to tuck in → ②

② Fold corner and secure

③ Continue down

④ Repeat to top and tie and fold over as before

⑤

N.B. Be sure to cover just below the knee to below the coronet and to leave excess padding showing.

STABLE BANDAGES – when used with overreach boots, give good protection while travelling. When used on their own, must extend down to cover the coronet.

Figure 8 bandage

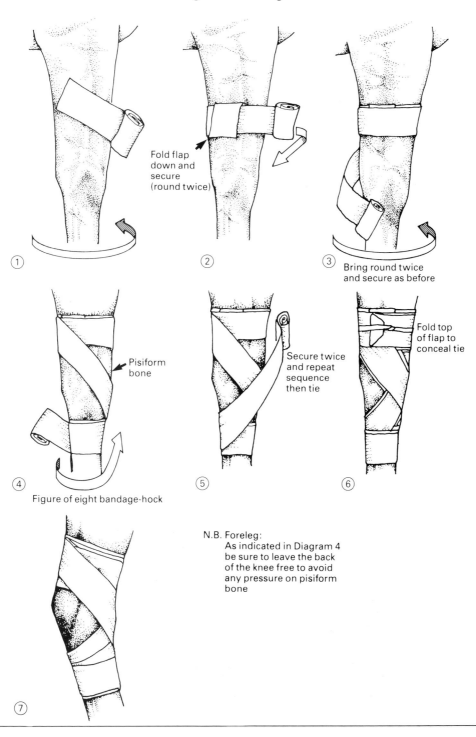

(1)

Fold flap
down and
secure
(round twice)

(2)

(3) Bring round twice
and secure as before

Pisiform
bone

(4)

Figure of eight bandage-hock

Secure twice
and repeat
sequence
then tie

(5)

Fold top
of flap to
conceal tie

(6)

(7)

N.B. Foreleg:
As indicated in Diagram 4
be sure to leave the back
of the knee free to avoid
any pressure on pisiform
bone

N.B. When *any* bandage is removed, it should be unwound and passed loosely from hand to hand, without trying to roll it up as you go. This is best done afterwards when you don't have a horse to contend with as well.

Bandaging for veterinary purposes

Any bandaging done for veterinary reasons should be explained, and demonstrated, by the vet if you ask him. One important rule, however, is that if you have to bandage a dressing on the knee for any reason, a figure of eight bandage must be used, and on no account must the small bone which sticks out slightly from the back of the knee (the pisiform bone) be covered by the bandage, as pressure will cause the bone to break through the skin.

When poulticing a foot, you can use crêpe or exercise bandage to hold the dressing in place, with Gamgee underneath the bandage as normal. You will find that the poultice is more likely to stay in place if the bandaging is continued up the leg from the foot, but don't forget to bandage the other leg as well.

Your Horse's Health

There are several excellent veterinary books available which go into diseases and ailments in detail, but to care for your horse's health and well-being, all you really need as a start are a sound understanding of the signs of good and ill health; a knowledge of first-aid measures for emergencies; a grasp of the basic principles of sick nursing; common sense – and, above all, the ability to realise when the vet must be called in.

Situations requiring immediate veterinary attention must be learned and understood since delay can often lead to serious consequences, and, in treating the horse, the vet's instructions must be followed to the letter.

Many drugs and treatments, such as antibiotics, must be given as a complete course over a prescribed number of days – even though the horse may appear to be better in the meantime. An incomplete course of antibiotics will result in the horse's system becoming immune to the drug, so that, if it is administered again at a later date, it will have no effect.

New developments in the field of veterinary medicine are being made all the time, and although advice from other owners is well-meaning, diagnosis and treatment should always be left to a qualified vet.

If you are new to an area, or have perhaps had no need for the services of a vet up until now, you should make enquiries among members of the Pony Club, local riding club, BHS, etc., to obtain the name of a recognised 'horse vet' in your area. Any vet is qualified to treat horses, but there are some who specialise in this field and their services should be retained if at all possible. Quite apart from the fact that they will be more accustomed to handling horses, it can often save you a lot of money in the long run since their wider experience with horses can enable them to make a more accurate diagnosis straight away in obscure cases.

When you have found a good horse vet it makes sense to stay with him – nothing whatsoever will be gained from chopping and changing from one vet to another. One regular vet will come to know your horse as an individual with its own little idiosyncrasies, as well as being able to build up a complete 'medical' history.

Since vets are extremely busy people, always make sure that the horse is ready in plenty of time for the visit – you really cannot expect the vet to wait while you frantically try to catch your horse.

If you think you may forget, write a list of questions you want to ask him, and make sure you fully understand any directions he may give you concerning the treatment. Again, write down the details if the instructions are at all complicated.

A useful tip is to keep a diary for the horse, in which you can note the date of injections and vet's visits, as well as visits by the farrier, dates and types of worm preparations used, amounts (and prices) of feed or forage purchased and, last but not least, any peculiarities noticed day by day in the horse's behaviour – for example, if the horse goes off its food or drinks an abnormal amount of water, any discharge from the nose or elsewhere, if it is unusually lethargic or excitable (this can be very useful in determining when a mare is due to come into season), if it starts to rub its mane or tail or sore patches appear on its body, and obviously any signs of heat in a foot or leg, stiffness or lameness – in fact, anything at all unusual.

Very probably, most of these symptoms will come to nothing, but if, on the other hand, the vet is called, one of the first things he will ask you is 'When did you first notice . . . ?' – he will be delighted that you can give him an exact answer.

Signs of good and ill health

There are some basic indications to look out for which will give you a good idea about your horse's well-being, although always remember that each horse is an individual.

A healthy horse will usually be alert in its expression; it should turn and look at you as you go into its stable, or 'perk up' if food is offered. In short, there should be some reaction as you approach it rather than none at all. Routine observation will tell you what is normal behaviour for your horse.

The eyes should appear bright and shiny, with clear whites, and the mucous membranes of the eyes and nostrils salmon pink in colour.

The skin should feel supple and loose, and the coat should look smooth and shiny.

The colour of the droppings will vary from golden brown to dark green depending on the horse's diet: hay and hard feed will produce the brownish colours, and rich grass will show in bright to dark green droppings. The consistency will also vary, but as a general guide the droppings should break as they hit the ground. When a horse is first turned out to spring grass, the droppings may be quite loose, but if they become almost liquid for more than 24 hours the horse should be brought in and the vet called. (Diarrhoea in young foals is extremely serious, though, and the vet should be called at once.)

Similarly, if the droppings are very hard, or they are considerably reduced in frequency or amount for more than 24 hours – much less if other symptoms of illness are observed – the vet should be consulted.

You should watch the horse as it stales – passes urine – and note if it appears to be having any difficulty. Retention of urine can be serious if left untreated, and sometimes occurs after a journey or long periods of work. (One way to encourage a horse to stale is by shaking up the straw underneath its belly and whistling.) Mares tend to stale more frequently than geldings, passing a relatively small amount of urine at a time – especially when they are in season; geldings tend to be quite shy about staling in public, and will often not stale in a horsebox or trailer – when they do stale, though, they tend to pass a large amount.

The urine should be yellow-gold in colour; if it is very dark or contains blood, the vet should be called immediately.

If a horse is unusually restless or starts to sweat for no apparent reason while in the stable, especially if it refuses food or has passed no droppings for an abnormal length of time, it must be carefully watched, as the signs could indicate the onset of colic.

Restlessness and sweating, together with a dull-looking eye, are signs that a horse is in pain; what you – and the vet – have to do is decide on the site of the pain; as James Herriot said, 'If only they could talk!'

The mucous membranes of the nose and eyes are another reliable indicator – if they are an unusual colour, something is generally amiss; a yellow colour suggests jaundice or kidney infection, while a bright red colour is a sign of influenza.

When a horse is unwell, the coat will lose its shine; it is said to be 'staring' and will look dull and patchy. A very sick horse will normally refuse to eat, or merely pick over food which is offered.

Anything other than a very temporary discharge from the nostrils should be viewed with suspicion, as it usually accompanies coughs, colds, strangles, influenza and other highly infectious diseases.

Even in this scientific age, there is still a place for instinct; if you know a horse well, you may sometimes sense that it is not quite right even though there may be no symptoms apparent. If this happens it is worth keeping an eye on the horse until it either displays some definite symptoms or returns to normal.

The horse's normal temperature is 100°–101°F (38°C), and is taken in the rectum. The thermometer should first be greased with Vaseline (but not at the end where you will be holding it) and inserted gently but firmly – make sure that you keep hold of the end or it will disappear. A rise of more than 2° is abnormal, and if the reading is more than 3° above normal, the vet should be called at once.

The normal pulse rate is between 36 and 42 beats per minute. It is a good idea to take your horse's pulse once or twice while it is resting, so that you know what it should be under normal circumstances. There are four points at which you can take the pulse: the supra-orbital artery just above the eye – you may have noticed this 'beating' if the horse has been excited; the facial artery, which is just behind the jaw bone; the carotid artery on the jugular groove; and the median artery behind the elbow. (A digital watch is a great help when taking the pulse.)

Pulse points

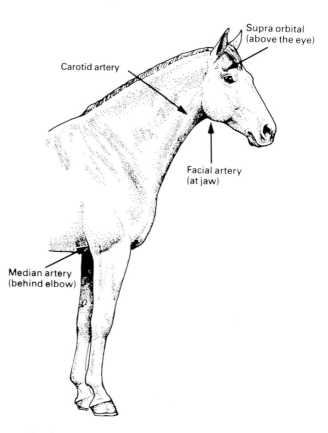

The respiration rate should be 8–15 breaths per minute and at a steady rate. Obviously a horse which has just undergone violent exercise will be breathing faster than one which has been resting, so this must be taken into account. Again, one or two practice runs are a good idea.

When to call the vet

The vet should always be called in the following circumstances:

(1) If the temperature, pulse rate or respiration are unduly abnormal, and there is no logical – or innocent – explanation.
(2) If the horse looks distressed.
(3) If it suddenly goes hopping lame and a cause (for example, a stone lodged in the foot or shoe) cannot be found.
(4) If a horse in work suddenly stops, refuses to move and breaks out in a sweat with a rapid increase in the pulse and respiration rate – obviously you will have to eliminate fear as a possible cause first.
(5) If it suffers an injury or wound which is serious enough to make you think it will need stitches, and/or you cannot stop the bleeding.
(6) If a horse is cast in its box (see page 73) or goes down and will not get up.
(7) If a grass-kept horse is found to be lying down and nothing will make it get up.
(8) If a horse goes off its food for more than 24 hours, even if no other symptoms are apparent – sooner if they are.
(9) If a horse starts coughing repeatedly – it could have something lodged in its throat, or have contracted influenza.
(10) If laminitis (see page 117) or colic (see page 115) is suspected.
(11) If the horse has a puncture wound and you are not sure whether it has been vaccinated against tetanus.
(12) If a young foal has diarrhoea, or an older horse has unusually hard, soft or foul-smelling droppings for no apparent reason.
(13) If a hot painful swelling appears on a limb.
(14) In all cases of lameness if the horse is no better after a couple of days' rest.
(15) If a skin disease, such as ringworm, is suspected since this is highly contagious and can be contracted by humans.
(16) If a broken limb is suspected – some breaks and fractures can be satisfactorily treated, but many cannot, and it is kinder to put the horse out of its pain and suffering as quickly as possible.
(17) In all cases of accident, injury, illness or disease if a claim is to be made under an insurance policy. One of the major conditions of all policies is that the vet must attend as soon as the condition is noticed.
(18) Finally, if in doubt, call the vet out; don't keep delaying in the hope that the horse will miraculously get better on its own – it is not worth the risk.

Wounds

Minor wounds and abrasions should be thoroughly cleaned with salt water or a weak disinfectant solution, dried and dusted with antibiotic powder or sprayed with purple spray. You must continue to keep an eye on any such wounds, and if they swell significantly the vet should be called as this is an indication that infection is setting in.

If a wound is bleeding heavily, obviously the vet will have been called, but you should try and stop the bleeding as soon as possible. The easiest way to do this is by applying pressure. Soak a pad of cotton wool in cold salt water and press it firmly over the wound – if the wound is a large tear, such as is caused by barbed wire for example, you will have to hold the edges together while applying pressure.

A pressure pad can be bandaged in place over a gash and should be left on until the vet arrives; if you take it off in the meantime to have a look, the chances are that the bleeding, which may well have been controlled, will start again.

A small wound on the leg should be hosed with cold water; this will stop the bleeding and clean the wound at the same time.

If an artery has been cut or severed, more drastic measures are required or the horse will bleed to death very quickly. Arterial blood will be bright red and will gush out in spurts, rather than in a steady flow. If this is the case, and it is at all possible, a tourniquet should be applied without delay (see diagram). A clean cotton handkerchief, folded lengthwise and knotted around the leg – or indeed anything that comes to hand in an emergency – and a stick of some sort make up the tourniquet, which is applied between the wound and the heart. The flow of blood to the wound is then cut off but the tourniquet must not be left tight for more than five minutes at a time or serious damage to the limb may result. If, after this time, the tourniquet is loosened but the bleeding has not stopped, it can be

Using a tourniquet

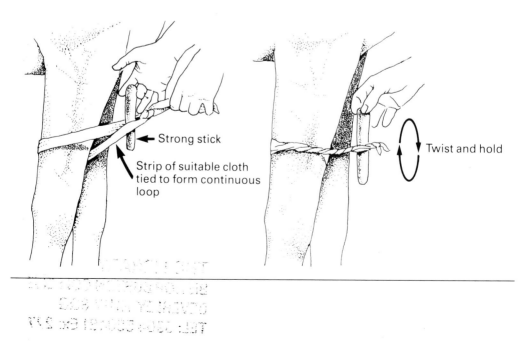

Strong stick

Strip of suitable cloth tied to form continuous loop

Twist and hold

re-tightened for another five minutes and so on. (If the bleeding has been controlled, a pressure pad can then be used in place of the tourniquet.)

Under no circumstances should a horse with an arterial wound be left alone until the vet has been; even though you may have succeeded in stopping the bleeding temporarily, it will probably start again if the horse moves at all.

Any wound which will require stitching should not have powder, cream or spray applied to it until after the vet has seen it, as this will make his job more difficult.

With a puncture wound, particularly in the foot, you should remove the cause – a thorn or nail, for example – but take great care to extract it in one piece; if it breaks off inside the foot, infection will quickly set in.

If the tetanus vaccination is up to date, the foot or limb is cool (the injury being very recent) and the cause is easily removed, you need not call the vet if the puncture is known to be relatively shallow. Pour neat hydrogen peroxide into the 'hole' to clean it out thoroughly and apply a poultice, changing it twice a day for three days. If there is no heat in the foot and the horse is not lame after this time, you can be reasonably sure that the wound has healed satisfactorily, but pack the foot with Stockholm tar and cotton wool for a few more days to be sure.

If, however, there is heat in the foot after the first poultice has cooled down, the vet must attend as he will probably need to enlarge the hole to allow drainage of pus. In severe cases he may pack the hole with thin bandage, leaving the end protruding from it; this is then pulled out a little at a time over a period of a few days, which ensures that a drainage hole is kept open.

(Lack of free drainage is the main reason why wounds to the poll or withers are potentially so serious. By their very position it is extremely difficult for the wound to drain – except inwards and downwards – and a relatively small wound can develop severe infection over a very large area unless treated straight away with injections of 'broad spectrum' antiobiotics.)

Overreaches are fairly common wounds. If the cut is small and not deep, clean it thoroughly, hose with cold water, dry and apply purple spray. If the horse is lame, but the wound is again small and on the bulb of the heel, poultice with Animalintex, alternating with cold hosing. If the overreach is high, on the back of the pastern or tendon, and deep, the vet should be called in case the tendon has been damaged.

Any horse prone to overreaching should be shod with the toes of the hind shoes set back, and should wear overreach boots as a matter of course.

THE LIBRARY
BISHOP BURTON COLLEGE
BEVERLEY HU17 8QG
TEL: 0964 550481 Ex: 227

Poulticing

Whenever a wound is involved, Animalintex poultices should be used in preference to kaolin (which are better for strains and sprains).

A piece of Animalintex is cut to size to cover the affected area, and then soaked in hot water. A good way of doing this is by placing the poultice, sticky side down, on a tin tray and pouring very hot water over it. Leave it for a few minutes to soak through, and then roll the excess water out with a milk bottle or rolling pin, tipping the tray as you do so to allow the water to drain off. Take the tray to the stable, together with a pair of scissors, a double thickness of polythene to cover the poultice, Gamgee, sack boot and bandages. The horse must be tied up, or held by another person.

Make sure that the poultice has cooled down sufficiently – test it on your hand – and place it over the wound. Cover it with the polythene and preferably Gamgee or cotton wool, put the sack boot (if appropriate) on over the top, wrap Gamgee round the leg and pastern, and bandage the whole lot in place, making a figure of eight bandage round the foot and continuing up the leg to just below the top edge of the Gamgee. Two bandages will generally make a more secure job of this, but you should start and finish each one in a slightly different place. All knots or bows must be in the usual place – between the cannon and tendon on the outside of the leg. Always bandage the other leg too, with Gamgee under the bandage.

You may well find that the minute your back is turned, however, the horse will engage in the highly satisfying game of tearing your handiwork to pieces. If you have done a good job, it shouldn't succeed, but if the horse persists in wrecking all your efforts, it will have to be tied up or muzzled.

The poultice should be replaced with a fresh one every 12 hours, or as directed by the vet, until either you are given the all clear by him or the area has remained cool for 36 hours, with no evidence of pus etc. being visible on the poultice for that time. (One major advantage of Animalintex over kaolin is that you can clearly see what has been drawn out of the wound when you change the poultice.)

Kaolin poultices are used more for sprains; the tin is heated in a pan of boiling water until the paste becomes runny, when it is spread on a clean piece of Gamgee, allowed to cool slightly and then bandaged over the affected area in the same way as Animalintex, but obviously without the sacking unless used on the foot to ease the pain of a bruised sole.

A quicker way of heating kaolin is to spread the required amount directly on to the Gamgee and heat it gently under the grill of a cooker; or alternatively in a microwave oven set on medium-high for a minute or two. Take care when using a microwave, though, since the kaolin will boil and spit if over-heated.

Kaolin poultices can be left in place for up to twenty-four hours since their drawing/soothing properties remain long after the poultice itself has cooled.

Another form of poultice – used for the foot – is made from bran, which has a good soothing effect on such conditions as bruised soles. It also softens and cleans the foot, which makes the vet's job easier when he needs to pare sole away or detect the site of a bruise or puncture.

To make a bran poultice, pour boiling water over half a bucketful of bran and mix well until it has a crumbly texture but is not soaking wet. Pack the bran into a polythene bag, and place this in a sack boot. When it has cooled sufficiently – test it on your hand – put the horse's foot into the bran and bandage the whole lot in place. Bran poultices should be changed twice a day. The main drawback to using bran is that horses are more inclined to eat it since it is basically the same as a bran mash.

Poultices of any kind must not be used over stitches – the stitches will not be able to do their job – or over a puncture in or near a joint as joint oils will be drawn out leaving the joint with insufficient lubrication.

Tendon problems   The tendons in the leg play a vital part in supporting the weight of the horse, and if they are damaged or severely strained the healing process is long and difficult.

If a horse doing hard or fast work suddenly pulls up hopping lame, you must in this instance fear the worst (unless of course the reason is otherwise obvious) and suspect that a tendon has been injured. You must immediately dismount and lead the horse to the nearest convenient point from whence aid can be summoned. If a tendon has only been strained in the first instance, riding the horse on will result in a tear or complete rupture – even if the damage can be repaired, in all likelihood the leg will never regain its former strength.

This is one case where prompt first aid can make all the difference to the horse's recovery. Obviously the vet must be called immediately, but in the meantime the leg should be bandaged tightly with crêpe or exercise bandage (with Gamgee underneath) from just below the knee to the coronet, making sure that the pastern and fetlock are well supported. This will help to prevent a large accumulation of fluid around the site of injury, and make the vet's job much easier.

Colic   Even in the best regulated establishments horses can and do get colic. In its mild form it may only last for half an hour or so and cause little more than mild discomfort to the horse – when the horse starts eating again and passes droppings, normally all is then well. In its acute form, however, it is much more serious and can indeed be fatal.

The first symptoms in both types are much the same; the horse will not be eating, it will look disturbed, it will keep looking round at its flanks and may kick at its belly. If the pain is severe the horse will break out into a sweat and roll repeatedly; its pulse and respiration rate will be markedly increased – in short, there is no mistaking the symptoms once you know what to look for.

The vet must be called *immediately*, and while you are waiting for him to arrive, try to keep the horse on its feet. If it rolls wildly in a stable there is a very real danger of it becoming cast and this demented rolling may also result in a condition known as 'twisted gut' which will be fatal unless diagnosed and operated on straightaway.

The horse should *not* be walked interminably round and round the yard or field until it is exhausted, as it will then go down and prove impossible to get up again. It should be taken out of the stable, lightly rugged, and encouraged to walk gently when the bouts of pain are severe. In between these, it should be allowed to stand quietly, and on no account should it be left alone. (By taking it out of a confined space you will lessen the dangers incurred by rolling.)

If any horse shows symptoms of colic and is not better within half an hour, the vet should be called, and *under no circumstances* should any form of so-called colic drink be given by *anyone* other than the vet.

Some horses are more prone to colic than others, but some of the more common causes of colic are: poor feeding – bad quality food, unsuitable food, too much food given at one time, too sudden a change in diet, too much water immediately after a feed, working too soon after a feed; large quantities of ice-cold water drunk when hot and sweating; sand swallowed along with the drinking water; heavy infestation of worms. Prevention in all cases is better than cure.

Coughs

Many horses habitually cough when first asked to work after having been standing in the stable, but they will nearly always 'blow their nose' as well – this is just a way of clearing the passages and is quite normal. (It is not so common among horses kept at grass in a dust-free atmosphere.)

Dusty hay or fodder will also make horses cough – one reason for dampening the feed – but if the horse coughs repeatedly, or seems at all distressed, veterinary advice should be sought, and the horse rested until his verdict is known.

Similarly, horses or ponies coughing repeatedly at shows or other gatherings should be given a wide berth – they may be perfectly healthy; on the other hand, they may indeed have equine influenza.

Horses which are coughing must on no account be worked, as the air sacs in the lungs will break down and 'broken wind' will result –

rendering the horse unfit for all but the very lightest, slowest hacking.

Broken wind can be seen by studying the horse's flanks as it breathes after exertion: instead of breathing in and out normally, it will exhale twice for every one breath drawn in.

Loss of condition

The answer for a horse which starts to lose weight is not always to increase its food, although obviously you should consider whether it is being overworked on an insufficient diet.

The first step is to make sure that the worming programme is up to date as a severe infestation will cause loss of weight and conditon while giving a characteristic ribby appearance and a pot belly. A sample of dung should be taken to the vet for a worm count, and if this proves satisfactory, by all means increase the rations and feed known fattening fods (see notes on feedstuffs).

If no improvement is evident after three weeks or so, a blood test will reveal if the horse is suffering from a virus, in which case the vet will advise suitable treatment.

It is also worth bearing in mind that horses, like humans, can develop allergies to certain foods and this will require a patient process of elimination to determine the source of the trouble. Loss of a long-term companion, stress brought about if kept confined when previously out at grass, or a vitamin/mineral deficiency are other possible causes.

Laminitis

Laminitis, or fever of the feet, is an extremely serious condition which, if neglected, can lead to the ultimate destruction of the animal. Caused, in the main, by too much rich grass, it tends to strike in spring and early summer and affects ponies and heavier horses more than Thoroughbreds.

Acute inflammation and breakdown of the sensitive laminae inside the feet cause the swollen tissues to press against the unyielding outer horn, giving rise to agonising pain. In time, if untreated, the pedal bone will rotate inside the foot as the damaged tissues can no longer provide support, until it finally breaks through the sole. Once these fundamental changes to the structure begin, there is very little to be done to save the horse.

The first symptoms are heat in the feet and a shortened stride, followed by an increased unwillingness to move and a tendency to shift uneasily from one front foot to the other. The characteristic stance of a horse with laminitis is unmistakable. With both front legs extended forwards, the horse tries to bear its weight on the heels – rather than the whole – of its feet. Prompt veterinary treatment is essential, and even when a cure has been effected, preventative measures will have to be taken for the rest of the horse's life. Once stricken by laminitis, a horse will be prone to it in future – the feet of

Typical stance of horse suffering from laminitis

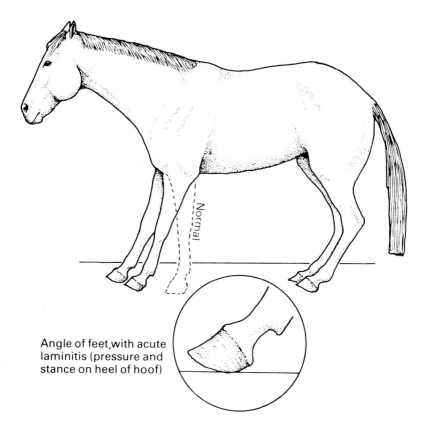

Normal

Angle of feet,with acute
laminitis (pressure and
stance on heel of hoof)

past sufferers have a tell-tale ridged appearance which serves as a warning to a prospective purchaser.

The grazing must be severely curtailed as soon as the spring grass is up. A 'starvation paddock' is ideal since the horse can still exercise, and an area of the usual field could be fenced off for this purpose (see Chapter 16 for advice on temporary fencing). Failing this, the horse must be kept stabled throughout the day and only allowed two or three hours grazing at night. Small amounts of hay must be given during the day, as it is not good for the stomach to remain completely empty for long periods. A careful watch must be kept to see that the horse does not gain weight and is well exercised.

Laminitis can also follow after other illnesses – and totally unrelated to grass – so the feet must always be inspected carefully.

Skin diseases

There are two fairly common skin diseases which will require both veterinary treatment and first aid – ringworm and Canadian Pox – which you should learn to recognise.

Ringworm

Ringworm can be seen as raised circular patches of hair, usually on the neck and shoulders, which will form round scabs. The disease is caused by a fungus which can lie dormant in wood for years, and is highly contagious among horses and humans. The modern treatment is by internal remedy, but great care must be taken to keep all grooming equipment, rugs, bandages, etc. – in fact anything which comes into direct contact with the horse – thoroughly washed and disinfected. Leather should be washed in water containing washing soda, and you must wear rubber gloves when handling the horse. Do not allow the horse to come into contact with others until the vet has given the all clear, and the stable must be disinfected and all bedding burned. Don't allow anyone other than yourself and the vet to visit the horse, or any of its tack to be used on another. If the horse is to be ridden – it is not necessary to stop work – it must not be allowed to sweat. A cotton sheet worn under a rug should be changed every day and washed – this is easier than trying to wash and change proper rugs, but the top rug must be thoroughly washed once the horse is pronounced cured.

Canadian pox

Canadian pox is often confused with ringworm, but the patches are usually smaller and do not have the characteristic ring-like appearance. The disease is equally contagious, though, so the same precautionary procedures must be followed. Both ringworm and Canadian pox can cause loss of condition in the horse, so veterinary treatment is essential.

Also coming under the heading of skin diseases are two parasitic forms: mange and lice.

Mange

Mange is a notifiable disease – to the police or Ministry of Agriculture – and its presence should be suspected if the horse shows signs of extreme irritation on its back, root of mane and tail. Oozing sores will develop accompanied by loss of hair, and the horse will be in extreme discomfort. It is highly contagious so the vet must be called and the usual isolation measures taken.

Lice

Lice are commonly found on ponies and some horses during the spring and summer, and are seen as small white specks at the roots of the mane and tail. They are easily dealt with by dusting with a proprietary powder such as DDT, following the manufacturers' instructions. Lice are rapidly passed from one horse to another.

Sweet Itch

Sweet itch is a fairly common – but non-contagious – skin complaint which affects the mane and root of the tail.

It is thought to be caused by tiny biting midges which flourish near water; they attack in the early morning and again towards dusk in the summer. The intense irritation caused by their bites makes the horse rub its mane and tail raw, and the resulting oozing sores in turn encourage the midges still further. Sweet itch should be suspected in any horse whose mane and tail develops bald patches in spring or summer.

The vet will advise on treatment, but you will probably have to bring the horse in, away from the flies, at these times in the day. Once a horse has had sweet itch once, it will be prone to it thereafter, and the crest of the mane and root of the tail will take on a characteristic 'ridged' appearance. Again, a point to look for when buying a horse.

Strangles

One other contagious disease not yet mentioned is strangles; it normally requires the attention of the vet, and is characterised by a thick discharge from the nose (the mucous membranes are bright red in colour), high temperature, coughing and a typical stance with the neck extended and nose poked out. As the disease progresses, hard swellings will be felt in the angle of the jaw. These are abscesses which will ultimately burst, and after this the horse will be much more comfortable. Any horse suffering from strangles must be kept away from others, and the usual precautions taken with its tack and equipment – the vet will advise you when all is safe once more.

Azoturia

This condition (which, along with lymphangitis, is also known as 'Monday morning disease') can strike without warning, and prompt action is essential.

Also known as 'tying up', it is connected with an excess of protein in the system and insufficient exercise; many horses will never experience it, but those which do will tend to get it again if their diet is not carefully monitored.

It is also another reason why a stabled horse should be worked in gradually before fast work is undertaken (i.e. start off by walking and trotting for 20–30 minutes before setting off for a gallop), as sudden violent exercise can trigger off an attack in horses prone to azoturia.

In its severe form, azoturia will cause the horse to stop dead in its tracks with its legs rigidly extended, or stagger wildly with an increasingly stiff back and quarters before lurching to a complete halt. It will sweat profusely and look extremely distressed.

You must dismount immediately, and summon help. If the horse is unwilling to move you *must not* force it to do so. No matter where you are at the time, the horse will have to stay put until the vet arrives to administer a muscle relaxant.

If the horse will walk, you can lead it slowly home, but you must stop at once if the horse wishes to.

It is a frightening experience for both horse and rider, and if it happens to you, be sure to ask the vet what you can do to prevent it happening again. If necessary write down all his instructions in case time should dim your memory. (See also the chapter on feeding.)

The basic precautions are to feed according to the amount of work done – if the horse is laid off for any reason, cut all grain and give bran mashes, meadow rather than seed hay, and put Epsom salts into the drinking water.

Lymphangitis

The other Monday morning disease, it is caused by much the same factors as azoturia – too much protein and insufficient exercise.

The legs will be swollen, hot and painful and the horse will require veterinary treatment.

Diagnosing lameness

Although in most cases the actual diagnosis of the cause of lameness will be a job for the vet, you should be able to recognise: (1) whether a horse is lame or not; and (2) which leg is affected.

Unless the lameness is obvious, you will need another person to lead the horse out for you so that you can watch its action carefully.

The general rule is 'down with the sound' – i.e. when the sound leg hits the ground, the head will go down, so if the horse is nodding its head at the walk or trot and the head dips noticeably when, say, the near fore hits the ground, it will be lame on the off fore.

In cases of hind leg lameness, the quarter of the affected leg will be carried higher than the opposite side, giving a lop-sided appearance, and the head will be raised as the lame leg hits the ground.

The horse may take a shorter stride with the lame leg (both in front or behind), or drag the toe. In many cases lameness in front will be more marked when the horse is going downhill, and hind leg lameness more marked when trotting uphill.

If the cause of the lameness is a bony enlargement such as a splint, the horse will be more lame on hard ground than on soft, but if the cause is a strain or sprain, the opposite is the case.

In order to diagnose the probable site of lameness properly, the horse should be led past you at the trot, on a long rope which allows free movement of its head; it should then be trotted towards you, when you can study the action of the forelegs, and then away from you so that the hind legs can be watched. If possible, this should be repeated on both hard and soft going if you cannot find an obvious cause of the lameness.

Having decided which limb is the culprit, you should examine it carefully, starting at the foot, to try and determine the cause. Remember that the cause of 80% of all lameness is found in the foot!

You are looking for signs of heat and/or pain – and, above the foot, hard or soft swellings in addition.

Unless instructed to do so by the vet (which is unusual), you must not ride a horse which is lame – even if the lameness is only slight – as strains, particularly, can develop into serious damage if you continue to work the horse.

'Bridle' lameness is so called because a horse which latches on to this entertaining ruse will affect lameness when it is asked to do work which it does not relish. Another form of this is shown when the horse continues to be lame long after an injury has healed – in other words it has got into the habit of favouring one particular leg.

Bridle lameness is notoriously difficult to cure, and also you can never be one hundred per cent sure that the lameness is not genuine. Your only hope, after eliminating all possible physical causes, is to stop doing routine work for a while and concentrate on allowing the horse to have some 'fun' rides during which you hope it will forget the habit.

A change of scene and/or timetable or a period turned out to grass may also help.

General sick nursing

If you are in charge of a sick horse, the basic principles are much the same as for humans, and a good guide is to treat the horse in the same way as you would like to be treated yourself if you were ill.

A very sick horse should not be left alone, but do not disturb it unnecessarily. Frequent, unobtrusive checks are better if a horse is only moderately ill.

Obviously you will be following the vet's instructions, but there are some procedures which you can undertake to make the horse as comfortable as possible. You should always check with the vet first, though, and *never* try out any home remedies, however well-meaning.

The stable should be well-ventilated, but free of draughts – it is much better to leave the top door open and put on an additional rug if necessary.

The bed should be of deep, short straw (so the horse can move around easily – long straw will tend to get wrapped around the horse's legs) and be shaken up frequently.

Rugs should be as light in weight as possible – it is better to have two or three light rugs than one heavy one.

If the horse has a discharge from the nose, this should be encouraged to drain freely by feeding off the ground, rather than from a net or manger; obviously, the water bucket must be washed out and refilled frequently.

The vet will be able to tell you if the horse should be groomed while it is ill, but sick horses often appreciate a gentle massage of the ears and legs.

The diet will be prescribed by the vet, but it will probably be a laxative diet – bran mashes, meadow hay, Epsom salts, etc. Do not feed grain to a stabled horse which is off work.

All medications must be given in accordance with the vet's instructions, no matter how inconvenient this may be. If the vet has stipulated every 4 or 6 hours, then that is what he means – even though you will have to get up in the middle of the night.

Most sick horses will appreciate peace and quiet, so if possible they should not be kept in a bustling yard. When the horse starts to improve, it may then benefit from being moved back to a busier environment where it will have something to occupy its mind. Horses on the mend can often be more of a problem than when very ill – just like some humans, they cannot understand why they are being kept confined when they are feeling better.

If the disease is infectious or contagious, the horse must be kept away from others and a careful watch kept on its erstwhile companions for any signs of the disease having spread – this is particularly important in the case of influenza, coughs and strangles as work must be stopped immediately when any symptoms first appear.

The horse's appetite will be a good indication of how it is feeling; very sick horses will not want to eat, and skimmed milk may be offered. (Water it down to begin with and gradually reduce the amount of water added as the horse gets used to it.) When the horse starts to get better, you may find that you have to tempt it with succulent morsels to encourage it to eat. Quartered apples, sliced carrots, handfuls of freshly pulled grass, boiled barley and raw eggs in the feed are all useful items, and, as they are of a laxative nature, will not do any harm – but check with the vet first.

The horse's condition must be carefully monitored; its temperature, pulse, etc., taken regularly and written down each time. If the horse seems to deteriorate in condition, the vet must be called at once; don't hang on to see if it will improve again, even if it is the middle of the night. An already weak horse can go downhill remarkably fast, and by morning it could well be too late.

Above all, use your common sense, and if in any doubt ask the vet to explain exactly what is required. He would much rather spend a little more time and have you understand everything fully, than risk mistakes being made.

CHAPTER 16

Looking After Your Grazing

Even if you only rent your grazing, you should still make the best possible use of it, and it is unrealistic to expect the landowner to do everything for you.

Quite apart from keeping the horse healthier, managing the grazing properly will save you money in the long run as feeding costs will be kept to a minimum; good grass can supply nearly all the food requirements of a family horse from April until October or November, and still retain some value through the winter.

Harrowing

Before the spring grass starts to grow, the field should be harrowed. This is normally a job undertaken by the farmer, but if he is not prepared to help out – even if you offer to pay – you will have to look elsewhere; many small farmers will undertake harrowing for other people on a contract basis.

Harrowing clears out any dead grass and aerates the soil, encouraging the vigorous growth of the new grass and preventing the land from becoming too compacted.

Soil sampling

The next step is to take a soil sample from several points in the field, and, making sure that each sample is clearly labelled, have an analysis done by the Ministry of Agriculture. This service costs very little, and the cost can easily be saved if fertiliser would otherwise have been wasted.

The basic analysis will show the pH value of the soil – whether or not it needs lime and if so how much; and the level of certain minerals – phosphates, potassium and magnesium – present. These minerals are not only required for healthy and vigorous plant growth, but a deficiency will adversely affect the bone development of young horses.

Fertilising

Lime and some minerals are not replaced by natural means, so if the field has been laid to grass for any length of time, the chances are that the levels will be low.

The nitrogen content of the soil cannot be measured accurately by analysis, as it will vary considerably depending on such factors as the stocking level, the time of year and the presence of natural nitrogen producers like clover, but an experienced eye would be able to give you a rough idea. If you do spread a nitrogen-based fertiliser, take care not to overdo it, as too much will 'burn' the grass.

When any fertiliser is used, check with the vet whether it is safe for use with horses. As a general rule, a period of two to three weeks should elapse before a horse is put back in a field after a nitrogen fertliser has been spread, but this waiting time can be reduced if there is a lot of rain.

Strip-grazing

If another field is not available, divide your grazing into two with temporary fencing to allow you to work on one side at a time while the horse occupies the other, and then swap over.

It is a good idea to divide the field into two or even three sections through the summer anyway; if the total area is limited, this practice will ensure a constant supply of grass for the horse by allowing one section to be grazed down while the other has a chance to recover and grow.

This will also help to prevent the establishment of large dunging areas. Horses will only pass their dung in certain parts of the field, and this encourages the growth of long, coarse grass which they then will not eat. If the droppings are removed from the rested half and the longer grass mown regularly, this will prevent the sour areas becoming ever larger when the horse returns. Remember that if a lawnmower is used, all the grass cuttings must be removed; areas of grass mown with a scythe may safely be left as these longer lengths will dry out rather than ferment.

Electric fencing provides a good temporary barrier, but it must be well visible and a single strand rather than mesh (see Chapter 4). It should be about 3 ft (91 cm) high – any lower and the horse might be tempted to jump over; much higher and a pony could well try to stretch its head and neck underneath. Most horses and ponies very quickly learn to avoid electric fencing, but nevertheless it should be of a type which will break under strain.

An added advantage of sub-dividing the field in this way is that you can use the vacant part for riding or schooling without being pestered by other horses or stock – or having equipment wrecked by your own horse when it is turned out to graze.

Spraying

Thistles and nettles should be cut or sprayed just before they flower, and if any spray is used where a horse is liable to graze, check with the manufacturer that there will be no side-effects. Several sprays have now been formulated which are said to be safe for use with stock, but always check first – and preferably with the vet as well. Spray firm representatives will normally advise on the right type and rate of spray for your circumstances.

THE LIBRARY
BISHOP BURTON COLLEGE
BEVERLEY HU17 8QG
TEL: 0964 550481

Cross-grazing

(See also Chapter 4.) If horses and/or ponies are to be the sole occupants of a field you should try to arrange the loan of some sheep or cattle to cross-graze two or three times a year. Not only will this help to keep the level of worm infestation down but such stock will also eat the grasses ignored by horses – thus saving you the chore of mowing.

It is better to have a lot of sheep or cattle for a few days rather than a few for long periods; the ground will not become so poached if the weather is wet and the disturbance factor will be kept to a minimum. Once the stock have grazed the field right down, they must be removed without delay as they will then turn their attention to attempts at escape.

General maintenance

If it is not practicable to remove the bulk of the droppings from the field, you should at least break them up regularly. This will help the hot sun, dry wind and frost to kill the worm larvae, and also slow down the establishment of coarse unpalatable grasses.

Once a week through the spring and summer, be on the lookout for poisonous weeds which may have taken root, and thoroughly check the fencing, repairing where necessary. Wooden gates and post and rail fencing should be creosoted once a year (only when they are completely dry), to prolong their life.

Re-seeding

If you own your grazing, or have a really secure long-term tenancy, and analysis shows the majority of the grass to be of little feed value, you can consider ploughing up and re-seeding. This is not a decision to be taken lightly, though, as it is a very costly exercise and in most cases expert management of existing grassland can be just as effective. If you do decide to go ahead, make sure that you have obtained all the advice available on the right time of year to embark on it, the best grass mixture, etc. (Clover, for instance, although good in small amounts as a natural producer of nitrogen, is very slippery when wet and will gradually overcome other, more useful grasses, while some of the fine-leaved fescues with their spreading roots will grow to form a springy mat which also drains well.)

The seed firms will advise on grass mixtures, but if you want or have to ride in the field to any great extent, it is often worth asking the playing field department of your local council for advice too, as they will know which grasses are particularly hard-wearing and will thrive in your area.

Making hay

Another idea which may cross your mind is to make your own hay. Although it may seem like a good way to save money, in most cases it is altogether too risky to contemplate unless a large acreage is involved – more than, say, 10 acres or so.

Successful hay-making requires considerable know-how, expensive equipment, best quality grass, good weather and a lot of luck.

Unless you own the necessary equipment you will have to rely on borrowing or hiring it, or contracting a firm or individual to do the job for you. If you only have a small acreage from which to take hay, you will probably have to wait your turn until after all the big jobs are completed – unfortunately, by then, your crop could have been ruined by bad weather. Hay has to be cut and baled at precisely the right time in order to be any good at all, and remember that it costs just as much to make bad hay as it does to achieve success. In the long run it is better to let someone else take the risks.

Other sources of advice

Although the Ministry of Agriculture do not normally make official visits to land other than agricultural holdings, they are pleased to answer queries and give advice on general management over the telephone.

There are also several booklets available from the BHS which set out the basic principles of grassland management and have been written especially for horse-keepers.

Advice can also be sought from farmers, but bear in mind that horses differ from other stock in both their habits and requirements – a field which is nutritionally perfect for cattle or sheep will not be so for a horse – but local farmers at least know the characteristics of their land and the basic principles of good management.

If the field is rented, the owner's permission should be obtained before any work other than routine application of spray and fertiliser is carried out as he (rightly) will want to know exactly what you intend to put on his land; there is no point in deliberately annoying him.

CHAPTER 17

Getting the Horse Fit and Roughing Off

Unfortunately you cannot simply take a horse out of a field and set off for a cross-country round or show at the drop of a hat if the animal is not fit.

Fitness has to be built up gradually, as for athletes, with diet and exercise to harden the legs and tone the muscles. Hard or fast work can then be undertaken without undue strain being placed on the heart, lungs and limbs.

Overworking an unfit horse can have dire consequences so forward planning is essential.

If a horse has been out at grass with no work for more than six to eight weeks, its condition is said to be 'soft', and a fitness programme will have to be worked out. It usually takes six to nine weeks to get a soft horse fully fit.

Two weeks before you are due to start working the horse, it should be fed a small amount of grain every day while still in the field – about 1–2 lbs (0.45–0.9 kg) – and sometime within this period it should have its teeth checked, vaccinations brought up to date if necessary, feet and shoes attended to and a worm preparation administered; you should also rub alcohol (or salt water) into the girth and saddle area every day to help to harden the skin and prevent galling. These measures will ensure that the horse is in the best condition to start work and that the schedule will not be interrupted.

The first ten to fourteen days should be spent on walking exercise, with only occasional trotting just to break the monotony in the last three or four days. The first few days' exercise should last about ½–¾ hour, building up to 1 hour by the end of the first week, and, in order to be of any benefit, the horse must be made to walk out briskly rather than being allowed to amble along at its own pace.

The amount of hard food should be gradually increased, along with the amount of grooming. Unless you intend to compete regularly through the winter, there is usually no need to keep the horse stabled, but you must keep a close eye on the horse's weight and condition – if it starts to go down as you increase the amount of work, or starts to sweat, you will have to increase the amount of energy-giving food, use a rug, and/or have the horse clipped. If the horse is to stay out, the grooming will be confined to a general tidy up for exercise, and the body brush must not be used.

During the third week you can start to increase the amount of trotting, but this must be a controlled, active trot and not a flat-out 'cavalry charge' along the road. During the first few days, the trotting should be done on grass or tracks, rather than roads, to avoid excessive concussion to the legs and feet.

The fourth week sees longer periods at trot, mostly on the road, and a few short canters. The horse should by now be on about three-quarters of its intended full grain ration, and the exercise periods may be up to 1–1½ hours.

Towards the end of the fourth week and during the fifth week school work can be introduced. You should not start this too soon, as circle work throws considerable strain on a horse's joints, particularly on the hocks. Two or three 10-minute canters (in a straight line rather than on the circle) will also help the horse's wind.

In the sixth week a half- to three-quarter-speed gallop over about one mile will give you an idea of how well the programme is progressing; if the horse sweats up and is blowing hard after this, you will know that it is not yet fully fit, so you will have to keep up the steady work for a week or so and then try again.

Jumping practice can be started during the fourth or fifth week, and again must be introduced gradually – particularly if the ground is unduly hard or soft.

The horse should be on full rations by the end of the fifth week, and you may find that you have to stable it during the day to prevent it from eating too much grass – a lot of grass has a laxative effect and will delay the horse attaining peak fitness.

If you are getting the horse fit in order to compete or hunt in the autumn/winter, it may have to be clipped as often as once a fortnight, but it should only be clipped once after Christmas to allow the summer coat to set properly.

Unless you have clipped a horse before, it is by far the best idea to get an experienced person to do the job for you the first couple of times while you watch – and learn. If you can afford to buy a set of clippers, and the horse is quiet, you could then attempt it yourself, but you should have someone with you when you make the initial attempt if only to hold the horse for you while you do the awkward areas.

Once the horse is fully fit, you will only need to give it a short gallop the day before a hunt or event to clear its wind; the day after it should be rested, with its feed cut down, and led out at a walk for half an hour if kept stabled. The feed and exercise is then gradually increased to peak in the few days preceding the next event, and so on.

Different types of clip

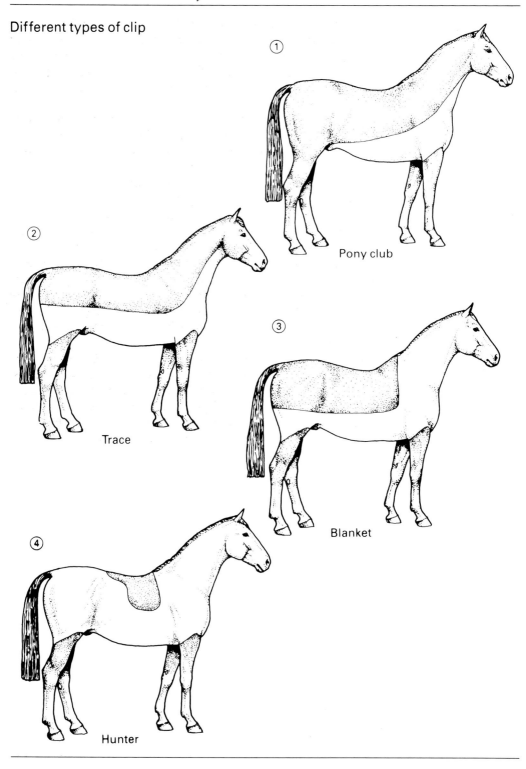

① Pony club

② Trace

③ Blanket

④ Hunter

You will find that if you school more than two or three times a week once the horse starts competing regularly, it will tend to get bored, and a stale horse will not give a sparkling performance. (This goes for jumping practice as well as flatwork – 10 minutes spent on this with a willing horse is worth far more than half an hour of battling.)

An older horse will generally take longer to get fit than a young horse, and one way round this is to keep riding it twice a week or so during the rest season instead of turning it away to grass completely, and also give it a small hard feed every day.

A stabled hunter or event horse must be 'let down' gradually at the end of the season – called 'roughing off'.

In the last couple of weeks, grooming should stop, the hard feed must be gradually reduced and also the amount of exercise. Depending on the weather, it should be turned out for longer periods during the day, and the warmth factor of its rugs gradually cut down until by the end of this period it is accustomed to having no rug on during the day, and a New Zealand is adequate at night when it stays out completely. Obviously as the weather becomes milder, the New Zealand can be left off at night when the summer coat affords sufficient protection.

The basic principles of conditioning apply in the same way to horses which are required to work in the spring/summer and rest during the winter. The only real difference is that clipping will not be necessary, and the horse will go out at night and be kept in during the day; horses working through the winter will normally be turned out after the midday feed but are brought in at night.

CHAPTER 18

Where to Ride, Road Safety and the Law

Unless you are familiar with the local area, you will need to find out where you can ride safely and legally.

Bridleways and tracks

One very useful addition to your library will be an Ordnance Survey map of the local area, which will show all the minor roads, lanes, farm tracks and bridleways. You do not need special permission to ride on bridleways (but make sure you know the difference between these and public footpaths upon which it is against the law to ride) but you must ask permission from the landowner before setting out on private lanes or farm tracks.

By law, farmers are not allowed to plough up or block off any bridleways, so, if you find that this has been done, you should contact the farmer concerned and ask him how long the bridleway will remain unusable. It is wise to do this before you take the matter further, as it may well be that the path will only be out of commission for a few days while the farmer is moving stock, for example. If, however, you don't receive a satisfactory reply, you can inform your local council and the bridleways representative of the British Horse Society, who will take any action necessary.

Although you have every right to ride along bridleways, do use your common sense, and if you pass through or close by any fields containing stock try not to disturb them unnecessarily. It is never a good idea to fall out with the farming community if you can avoid doing so.

You should visit the local farmers and ask which of their tracks you might be allowed to ride on – farm tracks are not necessarily public rights of way – and you may also obtain permission to ride in some of their fields at certain times of the year, such as stubble fields after harvest or grass fields after haymaking. Never be tempted to explore any lanes or tracks without first obtaining permission. Apart from being extremely bad manners, narrow tracks – especially in or near woodland – often have traps or snares set on them which are all but invisible.

If, on your travels, you see any stock wandering loose or injured, go to the nearest farmhouse and report what you have seen; it may be a false alarm but, if not, the farmer will be grateful that you have taken the trouble to tell him.

Obviously, if you have been given permission to ride on private land, aim to make your presence felt as little as possible; always close gates behind you, and don't risk damage to hedges, fences and growing crops by jumping from one field to another. If you are in any doubt at all about which fields do contain crops, either ask the farmer to clarify exactly where you may ride, or stay out of them.

If you find that other riders are taking liberties, and riding over crops or leaving gates open, etc., it will pay you to have a word with them to point out the error of their ways. Farmers are quite likely to ban *all* riders from their land without bothering to find out who the real culprits are.

Riding on the road

For many people, riding on the roads is a matter of necessity rather than choice, and with the increasing amount of traffic about these days, certain safety precautions are essential. The British Horse Society organise a special Road Safety Test for riders, and this is well worth taking.

Never, ever ride without a correctly fitting hat – preferably a jockey-style skull cap – even if the horse is the quietest imaginable. There are many people languishing in hospitals with serious head injuries because they neglected this most simple of precautions, and many more are dead.

It is a good idea to wear a warning tabard with a suitable message such as SLOW DOWN, PLEASE or CAUTION, YOUNG HORSE. These are obtainable from most saddlers and are a good idea if your horse is at all nervous or traffic-shy or if the road is habitually busy. These tabards, made from luminous material, help to ensure that you are easily seen as well as warning vehicles to be prepared for the unexpected.

Don't ride on the roads at or after dusk unless absolutely necessary, but, if you do, make sure that you have some kind of reflective clothing or a set of battery-powered stirrup lights.

Always thank drivers who slow down for you. Not only is this common courtesy, but also it will help to educate non-horsey drivers who may otherwise think that slowing down is unnecessary – your horse might be 'traffic-proof', but the next horse that driver meets may well not be.

If you can see a potentially dangerous situation developing, don't be afraid to stop the traffic while you sort things out; horses still have right of way over vehicles on the public roads, and, in any case, it is in everyone's best interests to prevent accidents.

If, while out riding, you are unfortunate enough to be the victim of a really inconsiderate driver, try to memorise his registration number, and report the incident to the local police as soon as possible. In rural areas especially, the police take a dim view of reckless drivers, and they will often deliver an official warning even if no accident actually happened.

The law concerning horses on the roads is, in fact, weighted in the horse owner's favour: it states that it is the duty of a vehicle driver to take *special* care to avoid a horse, and not vice versa.

If a normally well-behaved horse suddenly does something unpredictable like, say, shy into the path of a car, it is up to the driver to take evasive action – the rider is not held to be responsible for any damage which may be caused.

The only 'catch' is that a rider must take 'all reasonable precautions' to keep the horse under control, but having said that the law does recognise that a horse is not a machine, and it assumes that a driver will always have much more control over his vehicle than a rider will over a horse.

Warning tabards fulfil much of the rider's obligation under the law for 'taking reasonable precautions'; if a driver chooses to ignore the warning – or hand signals you may give to ask him to slow down – then he is entirely to blame for any accident or damage which may result.

Don't ask for trouble by taking a young or nervous horse on a very busy main road, though. Try to teach it all about traffic on quieter roads first, preferably in the company of a well-mannered 'schoolmaster' to give it confidence.

If your horse is inclined to shy at objects on the verge, bend its head to the right (assuming you are riding on the left) and use your right leg strongly to keep its quarters in to the side of the road.

A horse which is apt to panic when large vehicles come up behind it should be turned to face them. Flag down the approaching vehicle and find a safe place to turn in (driveway, farm track, etc.).

Straying

It is not unknown for horses to escape from their field or stable, get on to the road and cause an accident. In such a case, you, as the owner, will have to disprove negligence on your part – for example, that the fencing was in good repair and adequate under normal circumstances, or that a gate or door had not been left unfastened. Your insurance policy may cover you against claims for damage caused by your horse, but there are usually quite a few exclusions from this cover and normally one of the main conditions of the policy is that there has been no negligence on your part.

CHAPTER 19

Loading and Travelling

Before you travel anywhere with your horse, make sure that it is adequately protected, even if the journey is only a short one – an accident can happen just as easily outside your house as it can ten miles away.

Stable bandages or travelling boots plus overreach boots, tail bandage, poll guard, knee and hock boots and a rug may all be worn. (See Chapter 14.)

It is always a good idea to have some practice at loading a horse *before* you are due to undertake an important journey. If you do this several weeks in advance and the horse proves to be difficult, you then have a chance to put things right in plenty of time.

To begin with, make the interior of the trailer as attractive to the horse as possible, by having a good bed of straw on the floor (and possibly up the ramp as well), remove or open the partition (some horses will be reluctant to go into or through a narrow confined space but will be quite happy to have the partition replaced in its normal position once safely loaded), and try not to park so that the back of the trailer is facing into the sun as the strong light will dazzle the horse and make the interior of the trailer seem very dark and enclosed.

If you park so that the offside of the trailer is alongside a wall you will only have one side of the ramp to worry about as a possible escape route for the horse.

Have a small feed, or inviting titbit, on hand to give the horse once it is inside, but don't make the mistake of allowing the horse to eat it before it is loaded and secured.

Bring the horse to a spot about three strides from the foot of the ramp and then lead it positively forward, keeping alongside its shoulder; you must not try to pull it from in front as this will make the horse suspicious and it will almost certainly refuse to go forward.

If you have a long whip, carry it in your left hand and use it behind you as a reminder to the horse to keep walking forward if it hesitates. It may also help to con it into thinking there is someone unseen in a position to send it on from behind.

If the horse stops at the top of the ramp, it is usually better to let it

A HORSE DRESSED FOR TRAVEL – the sheepskin pad on the top of the headcollar is a poll guard, to prevent injury if the horse should strike its head on the roof. A tail guard, as well as a bandage, gives added protection if a horse habitually rubs against the ramp. The reins, however, should have been secured behind the stirrup leathers.

stand there for a few seconds before attempting to lead it right into the box. If you startle it at this point, there is a very real danger that it will throw its head up and strike it on the roof of the box, which not only risks a nasty injury to the head, but will put it off loading even more. Take a step back yourself, and send it on again – quietly but firmly.

Once in the box, make a fuss of the horse and give it a reward, and either ask your assistant (if you have one) to raise and secure the ramp, or walk quietly back past the horse and do the ramp yourself.

A lot depends on the habits of the individual horse, but, if there is a chance that it might pull back and you are alone, it is better to leave it untied while you put the ramp up. Pass the lead rope round the breast bar and keep hold of the end so that, if it should try to go backwards, you are then in a position of some control. If the horse is tied up, again there is the danger of it throwing its head up (when it feels the restraint) and striking it on the roof. In all probability it would then panic and pull back until free; thus learning an extremely annoying and dangerous habit.

Having secured the ramp (and breeching strap if the partition is in place) you can then go round to the front and tie the horse up. It must be tied to a piece of string attached to a ring, and must be on a very short rope – just long enough to enable it to reach the haynet and no longer. If the horse can turn its head right round, there is the danger of it overbalancing as you are travelling – particularly in the case of a young or inexperienced horse.

Make a final check that all is secure – especially the towing hitch – before you drive off. If you are unused to towing, remember that all braking and acceleration must be done slowly and smoothly; preparations for negotiating corners and junctions must be made well in advance as any changes of speed or direction are greatly magnified in the trailer. Abrupt movements can throw an inexperienced horse off balance.

Be particularly careful if there is a strong side wind blowing on to the offside of your vehicle; as any large or high-sided vehicles pass you, either when overtaking or when coming from the opposite direction, you will find that the trailer will be inclined to sway, so in these conditions it is wise to keep your speed down. A vehicle towing a trailer is restricted to 50 mph in any case, but in fact there are very few conditions in which it is safe to travel at this speed; usually 40–45 mph is quite fast enough to be consistent with safety. Don't forget that you cannot stop suddenly when towing; apart from the distress it would cause the horse, the trailer might well jack-knife – or even overturn – no matter how effective the braking system is.

Upon arrival at your destination, check first that the horse is still in one piece, and, if it is at all agitated, it is better to leave it in the box for a while to calm down before unloading.

If you are on your own, and there is no one around to put the ramp down for you, first of all make sure that you have everything you might need to hand – e.g. your saddle, whip, gloves, etc.: you do not want to be fishing around in the car boot while trying to hold on to an excited horse at the same time.

For the same reasons as when loading, it is often wise to untie the horse and slip the rope round the breast bar before you let the ramp down – again you will be in a position of some control if it tries to come out before you are ready (it cannot in any case get very far if a breeching strap is used), and there will be no risk of it pulling back and panicking. Front unload trailers make life a lot easier in this respect, and are now much more widely available, but don't undo the breast bar until you have lowered the ramp and untied the horse.

If a horse is genuinely frightened of the trailer it is often a good idea to park the trailer in the field – suitably anchored of course – for a while and feed from it. Not only does the horse then come to associate the trailer with food, but, by leaving the ramp down all the time, the horse will see that there is nothing nasty lurking inside. Once it is going freely in and out, you can start putting the ramp up and taking it for short rides. A few dummy runs of this nature will also teach it that there really is no reason to get excited merely at the prospect of going in the box, as it does not always mean a show, hunting, racing, etc.

If you have a horse which is *not* frightened but is simply being disobedient, and normal tactics to persuade it to go in the box have failed, in order to be sure of success you will need two helpers to assist you, who must first be thoroughly briefed on the part they are required to play.

Attach two lunge lines, one to each side of the rear of the trailer about 4 ft (121 cm) from the floor, and ask the two helpers to take up the free ends. They should then stand either side of the ramp about a horse's length from the foot of the ramp, keeping the lines parallel, while the horse is led between them. Once the horse is positioned at the foot of the ramp, the helpers should walk towards each other behind the horse and pass, so that the lines are crossed behind the horse's rump and the helpers have changed places with each other.

The third person leads the horse forward and keeps its head down.

LOADING – the crossed lunge lines ensure that the horse can only go forward – up the ramp. Ideally, there should be a third person at the horse's head, but these two people will manage quite adequately unless the horse tries to rear.

The lines should then be progressively tightened so that pressure is brought to bear directly behind the horse – if it should kick or struggle, the lines *must* be kept tight. The helpers, if correctly positioned, will be well out of harm's way, and by maintaining and increasing the pressure equally on both lines, the horse will eventually realise that its only option is to go forward.

I have seen this method used with some really difficult horses, and it has always worked if correctly applied. It is much safer, and more effective, than using just one lunge line as many people do, because it really does leave the horse with no avenue of escape, and keeps the helpers well out of range of flying hooves.

An added bonus is that, once a horse has been loaded in this way a few times, it will quickly learn that there is nothing to be gained by resistance, and just the sight of the lines being set up will often prove sufficient incentive to good behaviour; eventually you should be able to load it safely on your own.

Although it is obviously nice to have an assistant present while loading and unloading, you should try to practice the procedure alone from time to time – you can always have someone on call to come to your aid if necessary – as you cannot guarantee there will always be someone around to help. The horse should learn to accept this and behave properly; it will pay dividends in the case of emergency.

CHAPTER 20

When Things Go Wrong

Horses, as I have said before, are not machines; they have minds of their own and cannot be expected to conform to set patterns of behaviour all the time. As you get to know your individual horse you will come to understand the way in which its mind works – you will learn to recognise when it is genuinely frightened, for example, and when it is simply 'trying it on'.

The following notes on various disobediences are designed primarily as guidelines to possible remedies – they will not always work with every horse, but at least they should provide a base from which to start.

Napping

A horse which refuses to leaves its companions – a habit called 'napping' – can be a great nuisance, especially at shows, so, if possible, it should be cured of this irritating behaviour. You can start by arranging matters so that it is rewarded when it leaves others – a feed waiting in the stable, for example. When out riding, go in front from time to time leaving others behind; it is not a good idea to try and make the horse stand while others go on ahead – to begin with anyway – as this will encourage your horse to fret and pull. Try to find a route which will enable you to turn off, away from companions, on the way home. When at a show, if your horse refuses to enter the ring, circle outside the ring at a brisk walk or trot until you are ready to enter and then ride strongly forward into the ring from the circle without suddenly changing pace or direction.

In most showjumping competitions the first fence is jumped towards the collecting ring, and once over this make sure that you ride positively on and round the turn to the next fence. If the horse naps badly at this point and it is one of your first few shows, sacrifice possible prize money on this occasion and ride a fairly tight circle (about 10–12 yards/metres diameter) until you can push the horse forward in the desired direction. You will probably be eliminated for 'resistance' or 'crossing your tracks', but it will be well worth it in the long run if the horse realises that it cannot get away with it.

Shying

Horses which shy at positively everything, whether frightened or not, are best ignored. Older horses, particularly, may do this because of boredom or to get attention; varying the routes taken or the schooling routine will help to remove the boredom, as will frequent changes of pace. There is also nothing wrong with using your voice – simply talking to the horse as you go along, in a soothing or admonitory tone as the occasion demands.

Horses which are genuinely frightened, however, need tactful handling and nothing will be gained by trying to force them into submission. It can often prove wise to dismount and lead the horse past the object of its fright, with much praise and reward as you do so.

If you see an object or situation ahead which you think will upset the horse, *don't* tense up and shorten your reins ready for trouble. This will almost certainly transmit fear to the horse and cause it to play up, even if it had not thought of doing so before. Unfortunately this is much easier said than done, but you will find that the more you can relax, consistent with safety, the more co-operative your horse will become.

Refusing to go forward

A horse which is reluctant to go forward must always be ridden positively and this means a fairly strong contact with the mouth just as much as vigorous leg aids, perhaps backed up with a whip. You will achieve nothing by frantically kicking with your legs if the reins are flapping wildly.

Uncorrected, refusing to go forward can lead to bucking and rearing, both of which are dangerous. The only answer in both cases is to ride forward strongly – increasing the pace if necessary.

Refusing to be caught

Catching a horse in a field can prove to be an exasperating experience if it chooses to evade you – one reason why titbits as a reward for being caught are a good idea. Never approach a horse in a field from behind, either directly or obliquely, as this will encourage it to walk on, away from you. Even if it means walking a large circle yourself, always approach from in front, talking quietly as you come – an outstretched hand will also imply that you are offering something good, but keep the headcollar or rope out of sight behind your back. If a horse habitually refuses to be caught, you should turn it out with a headcollar on – but do remember that this makes life easier for any would-be vandals or thieves to catch the horse too.

If you are catching a horse which does not have a headcollar on already, you should fasten the headcollar loosely around the neck, just behind the ears, and then pull the noseband up into position before adjusting the fastening to fit properly (you then have the horse anchored while you do the fiddly bits); or, if the headcollar does not have sufficient adjustment for this to be possible, put the noseband on first and bring the headpiece over the poll quickly, holding the buckle in your other hand so that you are in a position to restrain the horse if it should pull away before you can get the fastening secured.

It is also a good idea to try and catch a difficult horse at odd times during the day when you do not intend to ride. If a reward is offered each time, and the horse then turned loose, it will not always associate being caught with work.

Stable vices

The main enemy of a stabled horse is boredom. This can manifest itself in several ways, ranging from mere bad temper to its most serious form of a stable vice.

Crib-biting, wind-sucking and weaving are the three main stable vices, the last two of which make a horse technically unsound if you subsequently decide to sell it, and all three render your horse an unwelcome visitor to anyone else's yard.

A crib-biter will take hold of an object such as the rim of a manger and begin by gnawing on it. This habit then leads to wind-sucking, when it takes in gulps of air with a characteristic 'burping' sound, normally accompanied by drawing in its head sharply.

A horse does not necessarily have to crib-bite in order to wind-suck, and the most confirmed offenders can sometimes carry on wind-sucking even when turned out to grass although this is fairly unusual since boredom is the prime cause.

These cases require a special leather collar which fits tightly round the gullet to prevent the horse arching its neck to swallow air.

Anti-weaving grille

Anti weaving grille   Housebrick method

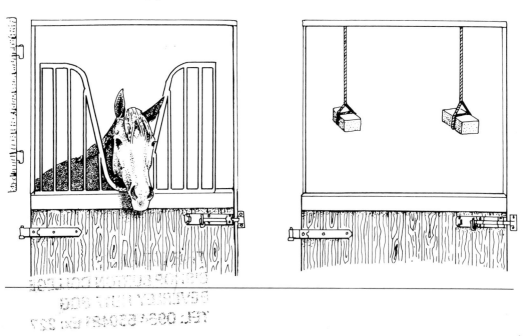

THE ELLESMERE COLLEGE
EQUESTRIAN TEAM USA
Tel: 000- 000000 fax 000

Normally, a horse which starts by crib-biting will graduate to actual wind-sucking even if it does not appear to do so straightaway, and for this reason any attempts to chew on or take hold of anything in the stable must be firmly checked. If reprimands do no good, you will have to paint a suitably nasty-tasting preparation – such as 'Cribbox' – on all the likely objects or fittings in the stable in order to discourage it, and try to turn the horse out as much as possible if frequent visits cannot be made.

Wind-sucking can, in time, damage a horse's wind and it is for this reason that a wind-sucker is classified unsound.

Weaving is a stable vice which is notoriously difficult to cure. The horse will stand – normally at or near the door – and sway from side to side, shifting its weight from one front leg to the other. This places a severe strain on the legs, and again is a classified technical unsoundness.

V-shaped anti-weaving grilles can be fitted to the top door, which stop the horse from leaning over and swaying, or an old-fashioned remedy is to suspend two house bricks on pieces of string so that attempts to weave are rewarded by a knock from the bricks (see diagram). It can sometimes help to provide a 'toy' in the form of an old football which will often keep a stabled horse amused.

All these vices are highly 'contagious' – especially among young horses – so offenders are never welcome in other establishments. This can be a real drawback if you intend to keep a horse at livery, since most reputable yards will not risk the habit 'catching on' and so will refuse to board a horse with such a vice.

THE LIBRARY
BISHOP BURTON COLLEGE
BEVERLEY HU17 8QG
TEL: 0964 550481 Ex: 227

A Last Word of Advice

There can be few subjects, other than the management of horses, which have attracted so many differing opinions, so it is not at all unusual to be given conflicting advice. Beware of those who claim to have all the answers – these people rarely do, and by the time you have discovered this for yourself, the damage to your horse has been done.

If you have a query about your horse's health, ask the vet; this is after all the subject in which he is qualified. Friends often mean well, but they could easily be misinformed themselves and so pass on erroneous information.

Similarly, if your horse has a behavioural problem, ask a qualified instructor for advice or lessons if necessary. This is what they have been trained to do, and since they will have seen and dealt with a large number of different horses they will be in a much better position to help than someone who has perhaps only had one or two.

Although some of the methods advocated years ago have become outmoded, many old-fashioned horsemen still have a fund of useful tips gathered from years of experience; advice from them on basic handling techniques is well worth heeding.

Although you will in all probability grow to love your horse almost as a member of your family, you must never allow sentiment to take over completely; horses are big, strong and potentially dangerous animals which must be made to realise that you are the 'boss'.

The secret of training horses, or any other animals for that matter, lies not in making them perform well, but in making them *want* to perform well, in order to please you. This is how the outstanding partnerships are forged – and how the most satisfaction is gained.

Useful Addresses

British Horse Society (Head Office for Pony Clubs, Riding Clubs, Horse Trials Group, Long-Distance Riding Group, Dressage Group, Road Safety, Bridleways, Welfare, Approval of Riding Schools)
British Equestrian Centre
Kenilworth
Warwickshire
CV8 2LR

British Showjumping Association
as for BHS

Farriers Registration Council
Mr B A Davanagh
PO Box 49
East of England Showground
Peterborough
PE2 0GU

FarmKey Ltd (Freeze Marking)
Universal House
Riverside
Banbury
Oxon
OX8 8TF